The Jaguar Smile

ALSO BY SALMAN RUSHDIE

FICTION
Grimus
Midnight's Children
Shame
The Satanic Verses
Haroun and the Sea of Stories
East, West
The Moor's Last Sigh
The Ground Beneath Her Feet
Fury

NONFICTION
Imaginary Homelands
The Wizard of Oz
Step Across This Line

SCREENPLAY
Midnight's Children

ANTHOLOGY
Mirrorwork (coeditor)

SALMAN RUSHDIE

THE
JAGUAR SMILE

A Nicaraguan Journey

PICADOR

HENRY HOLT AND COMPANY

NEW YORK

www.picadorusa.com

Picador® is a U.S. registered trademark and is used by Henry Holt and Company under license from Pan Books Limited.

For information on Picador Reading Group Guides, as well as ordering, please contact the Trade Marketing department at St. Martin's Press.
Phone: 1-800-221-7945 extension 763
Fax: 212-677-7456
E-mail: trademarketing@stmartins.com

Designed by Kathryn Parise

Library of Congress Cataloging-in-Publication Data

Rushdie, Salman.
    The jaguar smile : a Nicaraguan journey / Salman Rushdie.
       p. cm.
    Originally published: England : Pan Books, 1987.
    ISBN 0-312-42278-4
    1. Nicaragua—Description and travel. 2. Rushdie, Salman—Journeys—Nicaragua. I. Title.

F1524.R87 1997
917.28504'53—dc21
                                      97-794
                                      CIP

First published in Great Britain by Pan Books Ltd.

First published in the United States by Viking Penguin Inc.

First Picador Edition: September 2003

10 9 8 7 6 5 4 3 2 1

For Robbie

There was a young girl of Nic'ragua
Who smiled as she rode on a jaguar.
They returned from the ride
With the young girl inside
And the smile on the face of the jaguar.

ANON

Map of Nicaragua

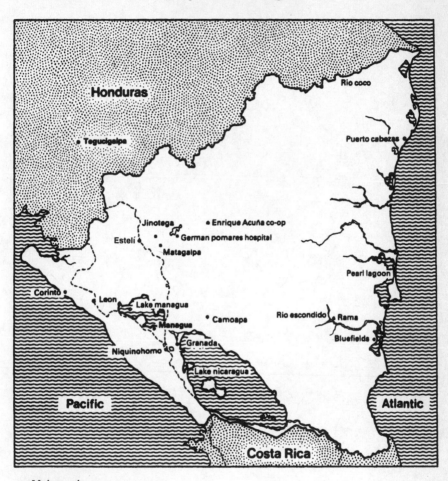

Main roads --------

CONTENTS

PREFACE TO THE
1997 EDITION

It's ten years since *The Jaguar Smile* was published. It was my first non-fiction book, and I well remember the shock of emerging, for the first time, from the (relatively) polite world of literature into the rough-and-tumble of the political arena. In the United States, then deeply involved in the 'low-intensity' proxy war against Nicaragua, the tumbling was particularly rough. After my publication party in New York, I found myself at dinner at a wealthy uptown address, surrounded by the *bien-pensant* liberal élite. Arthur Schlesinger, Jr., on hearing that I'd written a book about Nicaragua, embarking on a debunking of the Sandinistas that focused wittily on their mode of dress and lack of good society manners. This was a warning sign. If American liberals were so casually dismissive, conservatives were bound to be worse.

And so it proved. A prominent radio interviewer, in a live broadcast, greeted me with the question: 'Mr Rushdie, to what extent are you a Communist stooge?' The *New Republic* gave the book an immensely long and rude review, perhaps the most vitriolic I'd ever received. It turned out to have been written by one of the most important figures in the Contra leadership. I was inexperienced enough, in those days, to be genuinely surprised that a respectable journal should so brazenly abandon the principle of critical objectivity for the sake of some controversial copy. I am more worldly now.

In the last ten years, the world has changed so dramatically that *The Jaguar Smile* now reads like a period piece, a fairy tale of one of the hotter moments in the Cold War. 'The Soviet Union' and 'Cuba' are bogey-men that have long since lost their power to scare us. And in Nicaragua, the Contra war finally took its toll. A war-weary electorate voted out the

FSLN, electing, instead, the same Doña Violeta Chamorro whom I had rather caustically described in my pages. Daniel Ortega surprised, even impressed, many of his international opponents by accepting the voters' verdict. But at the same time, the Sandinistas were harshly criticized for pushing through, on behalf of many of their most prominent members, a last-minute land-grab of valuable real estate. (I have always wondered who ended up owning the comfortable Managua villa in which I was housed.) It was a characteristically contradictory Sandinista moment. When in power, they had acted, *simultaneously*, like people committed to democracy and also like harsh censors of free expression. Now, in their fall, they had behaved, once again simultaneously, like true democrats and also like true Latin-American oligarchs.

The FSLN sign on its hill overlooking Managua was altered, after the election, to read FIN. The End. In fact, Nicaraguan politics continued to be anything but straightforward. Dissension struck Doña Violeta's rag-bag anti-Sandinista coalition almost as soon as it took power, and on many occasions she was obliged to rule with the assistance of the votes of the Sandinista opposition. I had been struck, during my stay in Nicaragua, by the incestuous nature of the ruling class. Sandinistas and right-wingers had all gone to the same schools and dated each other. Now, it seemed, they were dating each other again.

But the stresses within the FSLN, what Marx would have called its 'inherent contradictions', did eventually arise to unmake it. During my visit I had been unable to meet the Sandinistas' military strongman, Daniel Ortega's brother Humberto, head of the armed forces. (The absence of any effective investigation of the hard-liners – Humberto Ortega, Tomás Borge – is a weakness in *The Jaguar Smile*. It seems probable that they were kept away from a non-Marxist like myself.) The differences between the Ortega brothers, and the group headed by Sergio Ramírez, whose key role it had been to persuade the urban middle class to support the revolution, became untenable. Ramírez left the movement, and the Sandinistas were hopelessly split. At the personal level, too, there were ruptures. Daniel Ortega and Rosario Murillo separated. Some of the people I had liked and admired left the country. The poet Gioconda Belli, for example, now lives in the United States. Her relationship with post-Sandinista Nicaragua is troubled and sad. And now a second election has been lost. Daniel Ortega has claimed that Arnoldo Alemán's victory was achieved by widespread ballot-rigging, but the independent team of electoral observers has ratified the election results. Now it really does look like the FIN.

In 1986, the story of Nicaragua looked to me like a David-and-Goliath saga. The Sandinistas, for all their incompetences and faults (and, on re-reading, I am glad to find I said a good deal about those faults), seemed like U.S. cultural mythology's quintessential little guys who stand up against the Mister Bigs of the world and refuse to admit defeat. It looked, too, like a tale of unrequited love. Nicaragua, which loved the music, poetry and baseball of the United States, was being crushed by its powerful, careless beloved. Politics is not often so poignant.

A decade later, romance has given way to what cynical commentators call reality: that is, the irresistible power of super-power itself. *Just do as we say,* as the White House emissary told Foreign Minister d'Escoto. Nowadays, in the epoch beyond the 'end of history', that instruction cannot be ignored. In 1986, Mario Vargas Llosa* had spoken of the silent majority of 'anti-Sandinista democratic Nicaraguans', a majority that then seemed more like a wish than a truth; now, that majority exists. Mario would say it always existed, and if I am wrong, then he is right, but one might also argue that it was created. After a long, hopeless war, people will settle for peace, at almost any price. Now that the economic blockade is over and the ruined Nicaraguan economy has begun its slow recovery, it is easy to blame the old rulers for that blockade. The power of super-power: first to describe a given leadership as unacceptable; then to create the circumstances in which it becomes unacceptable; and finally to obliterate the memory of its (the super-power's) own part in the process.

I met Sergio Ramírez in a European hotel room a couple of years ago. He seemed heavier, more burdened. I have corresponded with Gioconda Belli. It is plain from these and other contacts that the story of which *The Jaguar Smile* is one chapter has not had a happy ending.

*Mario, who has been a stalwart friend and ally to me, has this at least in common with Daniel Ortega: that they both vociferously opposed the death threat of the 1989 Khomeini fatwa against my novel, *The Satanic Verses.* I should say, for the sake of objectivity, that it is Mario's view, expressed on a French TV programme in which we both participated, that as I have grown older I have grown more politically sensible and therefore more conservative. I fear he may be right. I fear he may be wrong.

To re-read an old book is, inevitably, to have a sense of omissions, errors and regrets. There are one or two small howlers. In the account of the death of Julio Buitrago, I gave the impression that Doris Tijerino, among others, died with him. At the very moment I wrote this, Ms Tijerino was alive and occupying a prominent public position. Sorry, Doris.

I would like to have been clearer, too, about my difficulties with the Minister of Culture, Ernesto Cardenal. It was perhaps too polite of me to leave out the details of a speech I heard him give in Finland, in which he said that his beloved *campesino* poets were being given, as models, the poems of Ezra Pound and Marianne Moore 'in simplified form'; and in which he claimed, heart-freezingly, that Nicaragua was the 'first nation on earth to have nationalized poetry.' (A long-time literary opponent of the Soviet Union, seated near me, muttered, '*Second* nation . . .')

The whole truth would also involve a clearer account of the Sandinista leadership's strange susceptibility to the lure of international celebrity; more detail about the incompetence of much of their bureaucracy; more criticism of their treatment of the Miskito Indians; more, perhaps, about the widespread public dislike of the President's *compañera*, Rosario Murillo, and her grand ways.

These are the failings of any book written quickly, and in the heat of a passion. But even with ten years' hindsight, I stand by the fundamental judgments and attitudes of *The Jaguar Smile*, and feel, if I may say so, proud of my younger self for taking these 'snapshots' of that beautiful, benighted land; for getting more things half-right than half-wrong. And I mourn for Bluefields, already so poor when I saw it, and devastated since by one of the less-well-reported major earthquakes of recent years. I hope Miss Pancha the midwife and her pet cow are okay. I wish I had not run out of Flor de Caña rum. And I hope Rundown, the hot local band, are still singing *Rub me belly skin with castor oil*.

SALMAN RUSHDIE
1997

The Jaguar Smile

HOPE: A PROLOGUE

Ten years ago, when I was living in a small flat above an off-licence in SW1, I learned that the big house next door had been bought by the wife of the dictator of Nicaragua, Anastasio Somoza Debayle. The street was obviously going down in the world, what with the murder of the nanny Sandra Rivett by that nice Lord Lucan at number 44, and I moved out a few months later. I never met Hope Somoza, but her house became notorious in the street for a burglar alarm that went off with surprising frequency, and for the occasional parties that would cause the street to be jammed solid with Rolls-Royce, Mercedes-Benz and Jaguar limousines. Back in Managua, her husband 'Tacho' had taken a mistress, Dinorah, and Hope was no doubt trying to keep her spirits up.

Tacho and Dinorah fled Nicaragua on 17 July 1979, so that 'Nicaragua libre' was born exactly one month after my own son. (19 July is the formal independence day, because that was when the Sandinistas entered Managua, but the 17th is the real hat-in-air moment, the *día de alegría*, the day of joy.) I've always had a weakness for synchronicity, and I felt that the proximity of the birthdays forged a bond.

When the Reagan administration began its war against Nicaragua, I recognized a deeper affinity with that small country in a continent (Central America) upon which I had never set foot. I grew daily more interested in its affairs, because, after all, I was myself the child of a successful revolt against a great power, my consciousness the product of the triumph of the Indian revolution. It was perhaps also true that those of us who did not have our origins in the countries of the mighty West, or North, had something in common – not, certainly, anything as simplistic as a unified 'third world' outlook, but at least some knowledge of what weakness was like, some awareness of the view from underneath, and of how it felt to be there, on the bottom, looking up at the descending heel. I became a sponsor of the Nicaragua Solidarity Campaign in London. I mention this to declare an interest; when I finally visited Nicaragua, in July 1986, I did not go as a wholly neutral observer. I was not a blank slate.

I went to Nicaragua as the guest of the Sandinista Association of Cultural Workers (ASTC), the umbrella organization that brought writers, artists, musicians, craftspeople, dancers and so on, together under the same roof. The occasion was the seventh anniversary of the 'triumph', as it's known, of the Frente Sandinista. I went eagerly, but with a good deal of nervousness. I was familiar with the tendency of revolutions to go wrong, to devour their children, to become the thing they had been created to destroy. I knew about starting with idealism and romance and ending with betrayed expectations, broken hope. Would I find myself disliking the Sandinistas? One didn't have to like people to believe in their right not to be squashed by the United States; but it helped, it certainly helped.

꩜

It was a critical time. On 27 June, the International Court of Justice in the Hague had ruled that US aid to *la Contra*, the counter-revolutionary army the CIA had invented, assembled, organized and armed, was in violation of international law. The US House of Representatives, meanwhile, went ahead and approved President Reagan's request for $100 million-worth of new aid for the counter-revolution. In what looked like an act of retaliation, President Daniel Ortega of Nicaragua had announced the closure of the opposition newspaper, *La Prensa*, and the expulsion of two turbulent priests, Bishop Vega and Monsignor Bismark Carballo. The storm was brewing.

I was in Nicaragua for three weeks in July. What follows, therefore, is a portrait of a moment, no more, in the life of that beautiful, volcanic country. I did not go to Nicaragua intending to write a book, or, indeed, to write at all; but my encounter with the place affected me so deeply that in the end I had no choice. So: a moment, but, I believe, a crucial and revealing one, because it was neither a beginning nor an end, but a middle, a time that felt close to the fulcrum of history, a time when all things, all the possible futures, were still (just) in the balance.

Nor, in spite of everything, did it seem, as I had feared it might, like a time without hope.

1

❧

SANDINO'S HAT

'Cristoforo Colón set sail from Palos de Moguer in Spain, to find the lands of the Great Khan, where there were castles of gold, and the species were growing up in a wildly way; and, when walking on the ways, precious stones were frequently found. However, instead of that world, another, also rich, beautiful and plenty of fantasy, was discovered: America.'

I read this passage on a 'tobacco map' of Cuba at Havana airport, and to a traveller en route to Central America for the first time, it seemed like a propitious text. Later, however, as the plane wheeled over the green lagoon in the crater of the volcano of Apoyeque, and Managua came into view, I recalled another, darker text, from Neruda's poem *Centro América*:

> *Land as slim as a whip,*
> *hot as torture,*
> *your step in Honduras, your blood*
> *in Santo Domingo, at night,*
> *your eyes in Nicaragua*

6

touch me, call me, grip me,
and throughout American lands
I knock on doors to speak,
I tap on tongues that are tied,
I raise curtains, I plunge
my hands into blood:
O, sorrows
of my land, O death-rattle
of the great established silence,
O, long-suffering peoples,
O, slender waist of tears.

To understand the living in Nicaragua, I found, it was necessary to begin with the dead. The country was full of ghosts.
Sandino vive, a wall shouted at me the moment I arrived, and at
once a large pinkish boulder replied, *Cristo vive*, and, what's
more, *viene pronto*. A few moments later I passed the empty
plinth upon which, until seven years ago, there stood the
equestrian statue of the monster; except that it wasn't really
him, but a second-hand statue from Italy that had been given a
new face. The original face had been Mussolini's. The statue
toppled with the dictatorship, but the empty plinth was, in a
way, a deception. *Somoza vive*: chill, dark words, not much
heard in Nicaragua, but the beast was alive all right. Tacho was
assassinated in 1980 by an Argentine Montonero unit who
found him in Paraguay, but there was his shadow haunting the
Honduran frontier, a phantom in a cowboy hat.

Managua sprawled around its own corpse. Eighty per cent of
the city's buildings had fallen down in the great earthquake of
1972, and most of what used to be the centre was now an
emptiness. Under Somoza, it had been left as a pile of rubble,
and it wasn't until after his fall that the mess was cleared up and
grass was planted where downtown Managua used to be.

The hollow centre gave the city a provisional, film-set unreality. There was still a serious shortage of houses, and Managuans were obliged to improvise with what was left. The Foreign Ministry occupied an abandoned shopping mall. The National Assembly itself sat in a converted bank. The Intercontinental Hotel, a sawn-off concrete pyramid, had unfortunately failed to collapse. It stood amidst the wraiths of old Managua like an omen: an ugly American, but a survivor, nevertheless. (It became impossible, I discovered, not to see such a city in symbolic terms.)

People, too, were in short supply. Nicaragua's population was under three million, and the war continued to reduce it. In my first hours in the city streets, I saw a number of sights that were familiar to eyes trained in India and Pakistan: the capital's few buses, many of them donated quite recently by Alfonsín's new Argentina, were crammed to bursting-point with people, who hung off them in a very subcontinental way. And the roadside shanties put up by the *campesinos* (peasants) who had come to Managua with hope and not much else, echoed the *bustees* of Calcutta and Bombay. Later I realized that these echoes of multitudinous lands were as misleading as the tyrant's empty plinth. Nicaragua, which was about the size of the state of Oklahoma (if you turned England and Wales upside down, you'd have a rough approximation of its proportions), was also the emptiest of the countries of Central America. There were six times as many people in the New York metropolitan area as there were in the whole of Nicaragua. The void of downtown Managua revealed more than a crowded bus.

Filling the void, populating the streets, were the ghosts, the martyr dead. The Argentinian novelist Ernesto Sábato described Buenos Aires as a city whose street-names served to entomb the memory of its heroes, and in Nicaragua, too, I often had the feeling that everyone who mattered had already died and been immortalized in the names of hospitals, schools, theatres, highways or even (in the case of the great poet Rubén Darío) an entire town. In classical Greece, heroes could aspire to the status of gods, or at least hope to be turned into constellations, but the dead of an impoverished twentieth-century country had to make do with this more prosaic, public-park or sports-stadium immortality.

Of the ten earliest leaders of the Frente Sandinista de Liberación Nacional, nine had been killed before Somoza fell. Their faces, painted in the Sandinista colours of red and black, stared gigantically down on the Plaza de la Revolución. Carlos Fonseca (who had founded the Frente in 1956 and who fell in November, 1976, just two and a half years before the Sandinista victory); Silvio Mayorga; Germán Pomares: their names were like a litany. The survivor, Tomás Borge, now Minister of the Interior, was up there too, one living man among the immortals. Borge was badly tortured and, the story goes, 'took his revenge' on his torturer after the revolution, by forgiving him.

In a country whose history had been a continuous rite of blood for the forty-six years in which the Somozas had headed one of the longest-running and cruellest dictatorships on earth, it wasn't surprising that a martyr-culture should have developed. Over and over, I heard the legends of the dead. Of the poet Leonel Rugama, who was trapped in a house by Somoza's National Guard and ordered to surrender, and who yelled back, *'Que se rinda tu madre!'* (Let your mother surrender!), and fought on until he died. Of Julio Buitrago, surrounded in a 'safe house' in Managua along with Gloria Campos and Doris Tijerino. Finally he was the only one left alive, resisting the might of Somoza's tanks and heavy artillery hour after hour, while the whole country watched him on live television, because Somoza thought he'd captured a whole FSLN cell and wanted their destruction to be a lesson to the people; a terrible miscalculation, because when the people saw Buitrago come out shooting and die at last, when they saw that just one man had held off the tyrant for so long, they learned the wrong lesson: that resistance was possible.

In Nicaragua 'at seven years' the walls still spoke to the dead: Carlos, we're getting there, the graffiti said; or, Julio, we have not forgotten.

A painting by the primitivist painter Gloria Guevara, titled *Cristo guerrillero*, showed a crucifixion set in a rocky, mountainous Nicaraguan landscape. Three peasant women, two kneeling, one standing, wept at the foot of the cross, upon which there hung a Christ-figure who wore, instead of a loincloth and a crown of thorns, a pair of jeans and a denim shirt. The picture explained a good deal. The religion of those who lived under the volcanoes of Central America had always had much to do with martyrdom, with the dead; and in Nicaragua many, many people found their way to the revolution through religion. The versicle-and-response format of the Mass now formed the basis of much political activity, too. Sandino's old slogan, *patria libre o morir* (a free homeland or death), was now the national rallying-cry, and at the end of public meetings a platform speaker would invariably call out, *'Patria libre!'* to which the crowd would roar back, rather spookily if you hadn't shared their history, and if, for you, another, faraway martyr-culture, that of Khomeini's Iran, represented a fearsome warning, *'O MORIR!'*

The Nicaraguan revolution had been, and remained, a *passion*. The word had secular as well as Christian resonances. It was that fusion that lay at the heart of Sandinismo. That was what Gloria Guevara's painting revealed.

> *And then,*
> *we'll go wake our dead*

with the life they bequeathed us
and we'll all sing together
while concerts of birds
repeat our message
through the length and breadth
of America.

(From *Until We're Free*,
by Gioconda Belli.)

The generations of the dead were the context of seven-year-old 'Nicaragua libre', and without context there could be no meaning. When you stood in front of *la Loma*, the terrifying 'bunker' which had been the seat of the Somozas' power, you began to remember: that the first Somoza, Anastasio Somoza García, had presided over the killing of some 20,000 Nicaraguans until he himself was shot, at a ball in León, by the poet Rigoberto López (who was himself killed by the National Guard an instant later); and that, after a brief period of (slight) liberalization under one of Tacho I's sons, Luis, the other son resumed normal Somoza operations in 1967. This was Tacho II, last and greediest of the line. It was just seven years since the horror ended, seven years since men were fed to panthers in the despot's private zoo, since torture, castration, rape. Seven years since the beast. *La Loma* made the United States' claim that Nicaragua was once again a totalitarian state sound obscene. The bunker was the reality of totalitarianism, its hideous remnant and reminder. The beheaded, violated, mutilated ghosts of Nicaragua bore witness, every day, to what used to happen here, and must never happen again.

The most famous ghost, Augusto César Sandino, had by now been thoroughly mythologized, almost as thoroughly as, for example, Gandhi. A little, frowning man in a big hat, he had become a collection of stories. In 1927, he had been head of the sales department of the Huasteca petrol company in Mexico, when the Nicaraguan Liberal, Sacasa, backed by the army's chief of staff, Moncada, rose in arms against the US-backed conservative, Adolfo Díaz. Sandino returned to Nicaragua to fight on the Liberal side, and when Moncada did a deal with the US and laid down his arms, Sandino refused, so that Moncada had to tell the Americans: 'All my men surrender except one,' and Sandino and his 'Crazy Little Army' took to the mountains . . . Yes, that story, and the story of his betrayal, his assassination by Somoza's thugs in February 1934, after he had signed a peace treaty and when he was on his way home from the celebratory banquet. I was struck by the fact that it was Sandino's hat, and not his face, that had become the most potent icon in Nicaragua. A hatless Sandino would not be instantly recognizable; but that hat no longer needed his presence beneath it to be evocative. In many instances, FSLN graffiti were followed by a schematic drawing of the celebrated headgear, a drawing that looked exactly like an infinity-sign with a conical volcano rising out of it. Infinity and eruptions: the illegitimate boy from Niquinohomo was now a cluster of metaphors. Or, to put it another way: Sandino had become his hat.

In the west of the city was a low hill on which the initials FSLN reclined, each whitish figure about a hundred feet long, like a recumbent Hollywood sign. At first I thought the letters had been cut out of the hillside in the fashion of an English white horse, or maybe they were made of concrete, or even marble? But the sign was only wooden, made up of boards lying on the hillside, propped up, where necessary, by simple gantries. When I got closer to it, I saw that it had already started to look somewhat the worse for wear. Before the revolution there was a different sign on this hill. ROLTER, it read, advertising a local manufacturer of boots and shoes. That discovery intensified my sense of the provisional quality of life in post-revolutionary Managua. One wooden advertisement could easily be replaced by another. Nor could I resist the implications of putting the Frente Sandinista's sign on what used to be Boot Hill.

It was the rainy season in Managua; the skies were overcast. A cold wind blew from the north.

2

THE ROAD TO CAMOAPA

The walls of the home of Nicaragua's Vice-President, the novelist Sergio Ramírez, were hung with masks. 'Ah,' said the security guard, admitting me to a courtyard of old trees surrounded by spacious verandahs, *'el escritor hindú.'* Spanish uses *hindú* to mean 'Indian'; the construction *de la India*, which seemed OK to me, sounded stilted to Nicaraguan ears. So during my stay I became the *hindú* writer, or even, quite often, *poeta*. Which was quite a flattering disguise.

In Nicaragua, the mask was an indispensable feature of many popular festivals and folk-dances. There were animal-masks, devil-masks, even, as I was to discover, masks of men with bleeding bullet-holes in the centres of their foreheads. During the insurrection, Sandinista guerrillas often went into action wearing masks of pink mesh with simple faces painted on them. These masks, too, originated in folk-dance. One night I went to see a ballet based on the country's popular dances, and saw that one of the ballerinas was wearing a pink mask. The mask's associations with the revolution had grown so strong that it transformed her, in my eyes at least, into something wondrously strange: not a masked dancer, but a guerrilla in a tutu.

The true purpose of masks, as any actor will tell you, is not concealment, but transformation. A culture of masks is one that understands a good deal about the processes of metamorphosis.

I set off in the company of Sergio Ramírez and one of the nine-man National Directorate of the FSLN, Luis Carrión, to the town of Camoapa in Boaco province, to witness a part of one of the most important transformations taking place in the new Nicaragua. It was National Agrarian Reform Day, and in Camoapa land titles for no less than 70,000 acres were to be handed out to the *campesinos*.

Sergio Ramírez was unusually big (well over six feet) and heavily built for a Nicaraguan, and could look, at times, positively Chinese in a Mikadoish sort of way; Luis Carrión was of a much more characteristically Nicaraguan light, slight build, with a moustache that was – as they used to say in the Paris of the 1968 *événements* – 'Marxiste, tendance Groucho'. They were both remarkably free of the pomposity and circumlocution that were so often the stock-in-trade of politicians. 'How many acres have been redistributed since the revolution?' I asked, and once they had agreed how many *manzanas* (the Nicaraguan land unit) there were in a hectare, and we had all haggled about the number of acres a hectare contained, we arrived at a rough figure of over two million acres, handed out to about 100,000 families.

I was impressed, and said so. Ramírez nodded. 'It shows the people that we have the will to keep our promises.'

When Don Anastasio Somoza fled the country, he took with him everything he could carry, including all the cash in the national treasury. He even had the bodies of Tacho I and Luis Somoza dug up and they, too, went into exile. No doubt he would have taken the land as well, if he'd known how. But he couldn't, and nor could his cronies who fled with him, and so the government of the new Nicaragua found itself in possession of the abandoned estates, amounting to half the arable land in the country. The land being redistributed was taken from those immense holdings and not, as Carrión and Ramírez clearly felt obliged to explain, from anywhere else. 'Nobody who stayed in Nicaragua to work his land had it confiscated,' said Ramírez, who spoke excellent English but tired of it after a while and lapsed into Spanish. 'Since our absolute priorities are production and defence, why should we meddle with someone who is producing? On the contrary, we assist many large, private landowners.' On the road to Camoapa, which passed between the country's two big lakes, Lake Managua and Lake Nicaragua (really an inland sea, and the only place in the world where you could be eaten by freshwater sharks), they were at pains to point out farms and industries that remained in private hands. There was often a little, defensive something that would creep into the discourse of Nicaraguan leaders. 'No country is put under a microscope the way we are,' Foreign Minister d'Escoto would tell me. That sense of being watched, all the time, for the tiniest slip, made them jumpy.

The road to Camoapa was made of brick, like many roads in Nicaragua. Somoza used to own a brick factory. After the '72 earthquake he insisted that the nation's thoroughfares be reconstructed in Presidential bricks, which he then sold to the nation at high prices. 'But we discovered that the bricks were also very easy to lever up,' Luis Carrión told me contentedly, 'so that during the insurrection years we were often able to stop his convoys quite easily, thanks to his own brick roads.' Carrión looked too young to be running a country. Nicaragua made 'young novelists' of thirty-nine years feel antique. At least Sergio Ramírez was a few years older than me. Then again, he made me feel short.

I asked Ramírez about the recent pronouncements on Nicaragua by the famous Peruvian novelist Mario Vargas Llosa, in the *New York Times* and elsewhere. 'His positions have moved so far to the right these days that I wasn't surprised by his criticisms,' Ramírez said. What, then, did he think of Vargas Llosa's suggestion that the people who merited the West's support in Nicaragua were neither the Contra nor the FSLN, but the *anti-Sandinista democratic Nicaraguans*, who might even now be a majority? Carrión and Ramírez both laughed. 'There's no such majority,' Ramírez said. 'Let me know if you locate it.'

Vargas Llosa also hinted that the Sandinistas were a Soviet-style state in disguise; that the various nods in the direction of a mixed economy and a pluralistic democracy were no more than window dressing; and that, in fact, the FSLN was being obliged to preserve such things precisely on account of the pressure from outside. (Though, of course, he hastened to add that he did not support the Contra.)

Ramírez seemed genuinely annoyed by this suggestion. If it weren't for the war, he said, much more power could be given to the people than a state of emergency permitted; that is, peace would mean more democracy, not less. 'We have the right to self-determination. Our internal structures are nobody's business but our own.'

'But,' I suggested, 'now that the $100 million for the Contra has been approved, other people have made it their business, haven't they?'

Luis Carrión replied. 'The hundred million is not the point. The counter-revolution is not the real threat.' His view was that the Contra army had effectively been defeated. 'These days they try hard to avoid meeting us in direct combat, because of their heavy losses. They concentrate instead on terrorist acts, aimed at the civilian population, and at damaging production. We expect more of these now. We expect they will try something in the cities, even in Managua, now that they have the extra money; but we are prepared. They also have a major problem of recruitment and morale. Their numbers have fallen by several thousand in the past two years. No: the real threat is the CIA.'

Ah yes, *la Cia*. My reflex reaction to the Agency's entry into the conversation was simultaneously Eastern and Western. The Western voice inside me, the voice that was fed up with cloaks and daggers and conspiracy theories, muttered, 'not them again'. The Eastern voice, however, understood that the CIA really did exist, was powerful, and although it was easy to make it a scapegoat, it was also just a bit too jaded, too cynical, to discount its power.

The CIA operated in Central America through what it charmingly referred to as UCLAs: Unilaterally Controlled Latino Assets. Now that it was to be permitted to resume overt operations, those Assets would be going to work with a will. Conservative estimates of the CIA's planned 1986–87 budget against Nicaragua suggested a figure somewhere in the near vicinity of $400 million – four times the aid allocated to the Contra forces. Add to that the $300 million being spent by the Reagan administration to try and 'buy off' Nicaragua's neighbours, and you had a grand total of $800 million being spent on dirty tricks and destabilization, to bring to heel a country of under three million people.

(The total amount of money raised by the Band Aid, Sport Aid and Live Aid events, just to offer some sort of comparison, was less than a quarter of this figure.)

It was the CIA that had mined the harbour at Corinto, and in the face of overt operations like that, the Nicaraguan government would face real problems. Carrión said, 'Against such aggression, there is simply not much we can do. We lack the resources.'

Carrión believed that when Reagan realized the Contra would never do the job for him, a direct US invasion on some pretext or other would follow. I was to discover that this was the more or less unanimous opinion of the Sandinista leaders I encountered. 'Reagan has invested too much personal prestige in the Nicaragua issue to leave office without trying to smash us,' Ramírez said. The government was preparing for the US invasion by arming the *campesinos*. 'Our best defence,' Luis Carrión told me, 'is the people in arms.' It was a phrase I heard many times during my stay. Many thousands of ordinary Nicaraguans had already been given AK-47 automatic rifles, as well as other hardware. If the the Pentagon could be convinced that the US body count would be high, it might make an attack politically unsaleable. 'Nicaragua will not be like Grenada for them,' Luis Carrión said. 'It will not be quick.'

I had begun to see great mountains of corpses in my mind's eye. I changed the subject, and asked Sergio Ramírez about a recent report by the 'International League for Human Rights', published in the *Herald Tribune*. 'Repression in Nicaragua is not as conspicuous or as bloody as in other parts of Central America,' said Nina H. Shea, programme director of the 'New York-based' group. 'But it is more insidious and systematic.'

Ramírez began by saying that the most important human rights organizations had given Nicaragua a pretty clean report. Then he lost his temper. 'You see,' he cried, 'if we do not murder and torture people as they do in Salvador, it just proves that we are so fiendishly subtle.'

A cow strolled across the road and the driver braked violently. Ahead of us, the security outriders, who all, rather unusually, wore bright orange washing-up gloves, came to a halt. 'One must understand one's animals,' Luis Carrión said mildly. 'A cow will never deviate from its chosen direction, never turn around. A dog, however, is unreliable.'

We arrived in Camoapa, which was in holiday mood. Five thousand *campesinos* filled the main square, around which fluttered great hosts of small blue-and-white national flags, alternating with the red-and-black banners of the Frente. Straw Sandino-hats, scrubbed children in their best clothes, militiamen on guard. 'Señor Reagan,' read a placard held up by a member of the Heroes and Martyrs of the First of May 1986 Co-operative, 'you won't get even the smallest lump of our land.' And, elsewhere in the crowd, another banner demanded: '*Trabajo y fusiles!*' Work and rifles. It wasn't easy to believe in Vargas Llosa's hypothetical anti-Sandinista majority here. The government, understanding that its power base lay with the *campesinos*, had given rural areas such as this priority over the cities in terms of the allocation of the country's scarce resources. Food shortages weren't nearly as acute here as they were getting to be in Managua, Granada and León; and such preferential policies, coupled with the land reforms, had ensured that communities such as Camoapa had remained loyal FSLN strongholds.

Jaime Wheelock, another of the FSLN's nine *comandantes de la revolución*, who was now the agriculture minister and looked even younger than Luis Carrión, addressed the crowd. It was impossible not to notice that the emotional distance between the audience and the orator was very small. I couldn't think of a Western politician who could have spoken so intimately to such a crowd. The parish priest of Camoapa, Father Alfonso Alvarado Lugo, also spoke. 'I am happy,' he told the *campesinos*, 'that you, who used to be on the streets, can now cultivate the land.' The *campesinos* came up and received their land titles, informally, with little fuss. It seemed natural to be moved.

The versicle-and-response format took over. A young Sandinista woman acted as cheerleader. 'The people united,' she cried into a microphone, and the crowd replied: '. . . will never be defeated!'

'Let us struggle!'

'. . . For peace!'

'*Venceremos!*'

'*No pasarán.*'

Oh, by the way: at the end of the ceremony, the village band played – amongst other popular local tunes – the *Internationale*.

3

⸎

POETS ON THE DAY OF JOY

On the seventh anniversary of Somoza's departure with coffins and coffers, I found myself accompanying a well-known poet who was on his way to make an important telephone call. The poet was Daniel Ortega, whose most popular work was perhaps the one entitled *I missed Managua in mini-skirts*. When Managuan hemlines rose above the knee, Ortega was in jail.

President Ortega – or 'Comandante Daniel', as he was universally known – didn't want to talk about his prison experiences any more. His poem, *In the Prison*, indicated why this might be:

> *Kick him this way, like this,*
> *in the balls, in the face, in the ribs.*
> *Pass me the hot iron, the billy-club.*
> *Talk! Talk, you son-of-a-bitch,*
> *try salt water,*
> *ta-a-alk, we don't want to mess you up.*

I began to ask him about his writing, but he seemed embarrassed by my questions. 'In Nicaragua,' he said, 'everybody is considered to be a poet until he proves to the contrary.' Nowadays, his main literary effort was to persuade his ministers and officials to speak clearly to the people. 'Too often we fall into using a language that puts them off, that creates a gulf.' He looked like a bookworm who had done a body-building course; his manner, too, combined a bespectacled blinking, mild-voiced diffidence with an absolutely contradictory self-confidence. You wouldn't kick sand into his face any more.

Talking to the people was a priority for his administration. He regularly took his entire cabinet to meet the people in popular forums, making himself accountable in a way his main Western critics never would. I tried to imagine Ronald Reagan or Margaret Thatcher agreeing to submit themselves to a monthly grilling by members of the public, and failed.

Today, however, was about a different kind of communication. The phone call Ortega was on his way to make represented the ceremonial inauguration of the 'Inter-Sputnik' communications link between Nicaragua and the countries of the socialist bloc. We arrived at the dish antenna, which sat in the Managua hills not far from the wooden FSLN sign, and listened to speeches from Russian dignitaries. The new installation had been paid for by the USSR, and the US was already calling it a spy base. It looked like a telephone system to me.

As Daniel Ortega telephoned first his ambassador in Havana and then Nicaragua's man in Moscow, the stupidity of US policy seemed glaringly obvious. In Nicaragua, there were old Jack Nicholson movies on the television, Coca-Cola did great business, the people listened to Madonna on the radio, singing about *living in a material world/and I am a material girl*; baseball was a national obsession, and people spoke with pride of the number of Nicaraguans who had made the major leagues in the United States. In the old Somoza days, when the newspapers were censored, they would print photographs of Marilyn Monroe and other Hollywood movie stars in place of the banned articles, creating what may be a unique alliance of Hollywood with radical protest. In Nicaraguan literature, too, the US influence was of enormous importance. The country's poetry had been profoundly affected by the work of Walt Whitman and Ezra Pound.

Now, however, there was the economic blockade. A shipment of Dutch cranes, en route to Nicaragua, had been impounded by the US authorities in the Canal Zone. IBM had withdrawn all service facilities from Nicaragua, obliging an already impoverished country to change, at great expense, from IBM computers to other, less ideologically motivated brands. (What would become, I wondered, of the IBM word processor Sergio Ramírez had shown me with all the eagerness and pride of a new-technology nut?) Most recently, Oxfam America had been prevented by the Reagan administration from sending a $41,000 shipment of seeds, hoes and farm equipment to Nicaragua.

It was impossible to spend even a day in Nicaragua without becoming aware of the huge and unrelenting pressure being exerted on the country by the giant standing on its northern frontier. It was a pressure that informed every minute of every day.

In the morning paper, Nicaragua's leading cartoonist, Roger, had drawn a gigantic Uncle Sam, who was bending over and peering through binoculars at a tiny Nicaraguan house the size and shape of Snoopy's dog kennel. 'Yes,' read his speech balloon, 'I can see it clearly: they're definitely planning to invade.'

The 'Peanuts' strip, by chance, had just run an American variation on the same theme. Linus, Snoopy, and, if memory serves, Lucy sat watching TV, dressed up in camouflage combat fatigues. 'What's he saying now?' the girl asked. Linus replied, 'The same thing he said yesterday. He says there are people out there who want to destroy our way of life.' 'I don't trust him,' said Lucy or Patty or whoever it was. 'Really? Why is that?' 'I don't trust anybody.'

The Soviet ministers stood beside Daniel Ortega as he made his call to Moscow. The *New York Times*, in a leader article, had just called the Sandinistas 'Stalinists'. Stephen Kinzer, the paper's man in Managua, had belatedly filed a report (without visiting the scene) on the most recent Contra atrocity, the mining of a road in northern Jinotega province, near Bocay. The mine had blown up a bus and killed thirty-two civilians, including several schoolchildren. Kinzer's report suggested that the FSLN could have planted the mine itself, in a bid to gain international sympathy.

Pressure, and a phone call to Moscow. My enemy's enemy becomes, eventually, my friend.

There was a shortage of beans in Managua. (Imagine Italy running out of pasta.) Some days it was hard to get corn to make tortillas. Inflation was close to 500%, and prices had gone crazy. It could cost you six head of cattle to get your truck serviced.

The economy was hugely dependent on imports. Nicaragua produced no glass, no paper, no metal. It was also very vulnerable to attack. The economist Paul Oquist described it to me as a 'one of everything economy' – one deep-water port, one oil refinery, one international airport. US 'surgical strikes' would have little difficulty in paralysing the country. 'Maybe they would spare the refinery,' said Oquist, a *norteamericano* himself, 'because it's run by Exxon.'

In the five years of the war, the Nicaraguan economy had

suffered an estimated $2 billion-worth of damage. In 1985, Nicaragua's total exports had been valued at $300 million; imports ran at $900 million. Two billion dollars was roughly the same as one year's gross national product. So Nicaragua had lost one entire year's production in the last five, with most of the damage occurring in the second half of that period.

When the International Court at the Hague ruled against the US, it also upheld Nicaragua's claim that the US was liable to pay reparation for the economic damage. The Court also rejected the US argument that Nicaragua was the 'regional aggressor', and that states in the zone were therefore entitled to defend themselves against it. (The judges who voted for the majority verdict came from Algeria, Argentina, Brazil, China, France (two), India, Italy, Nigeria, Norway, Poland and Senegal. The three who dissented from the judgment were from the United States, Britain and Japan.)

The Reagan administration wasn't interested in international law, at least not when its custodians found against the US. The situation was surreal: the country that was in fact acting illegally, that was the outlaw, was hurling such epithets as *totalitarian*, *tyrannous* and *Stalinist* at the elected government of a country that hadn't broken any laws at all; the bandit was posing as the sheriff.

Daniel Ortega finished talking to Moscow and put down the phone. Everybody, Russians, Nicaraguans, *escritor hindú*, burst into smiles. It was, after all, the Day of Joy.

And after the Day, the Night. In a large, green circus-tent donated by Cuba, musicians from all over Central America were playing in a festival of contemporary music, the *nueva canción*. Salsa-rhythms and protest songs alternated. Managua had become quite a centre for liberal American musicians. As well as the artists in the circus tent, the *Carpa Nacional*, there had been recent concert performances here by Peter, Paul and Mary. Jackson Browne had been down, too.

Meanwhile, across town, seven women poets were reciting in the ruins of the Grand Hotel. Most of the hotel had collapsed in the earthquake. What remained – a central court-yard overlooked by balconies and open, now, to the sky – served the city as a cultural centre. The ruins were crowded with poetry-lovers. I did not think I had ever seen a people, even in India and Pakistan where poets were revered, who valued poetry as much as the Nicaraguans. At the back of the open stage, the seven women clustered and paced, all dressed up to the nines for the occasion, and all clearly nervous. They came forward in turn, to be introduced by the critic Ileana Rodríguez, and as each poet finished her reading and returned to the far end of the ruins, the others would group around her, to embrace and to reassure.

Two of the seven poets particularly caught my attention: Vidaluz Meneses, a slight, grave woman with a quietness of delivery that was gently impressive, and Gioconda Belli, winner of the prestigious Casa de las Américas prize. Her poetry was at once extremely sensual and politically direct.

Vidaluz Meneses' father had been a General in Somoza's National Guard and had eventually been assassinated by the Guerrilla Army of the Poor, in Guatemala in 1978. (He was there as Somoza's ambassador.) Her moving poem, *Last postcard for my father, General Meneses*, showed her to be a writer whose work had been enriched, though also made much more painful, by the ambiguity of her family circumstances. (At the time of her father's death, and for some years previously, she had been working secretly with the Frente. When her father found out, relations between the two became, not unnaturally, rather difficult.) In an interview with Margaret Randall, Meneses talked about that ambiguity: 'I have never been able to hate the enemy, but I feel a tremendous sorrow. Because someone I loved so much didn't share my ideals. And that, I guess, is the central thread of my work . . . And yet I know that with that poem I disappoint many friends . . . Maybe the poem seems weak to them. I believe that poetry has to be authentic, though.'

She spoke of belonging to a 'sacrificed generation', for whom the work of rebuilding the nation had to take priority over their private needs as poets. It was the kind of state-ment one might perhaps have expected from a woman whose revolutionary motivation was essentially religious in origin, as Meneses' certainly was. But Gioconda Belli, a far more secular poet, made very similar remarks to Margaret Randall. She had just decided, she said, to make her work (for the revolution) 'the best poem I can write.'

Belli's poems closed the evening. She had created a kind of public love-poetry that came closer, I thought, to expressing the passion of Nicaragua than anything I had yet heard:

> *Rivers run through me*
> *mountains bore into my body*
> *and the geography of this country*
> *begins forming in me*
> *turning me into lakes, chasms, ravines,*
> *earth for sowing love*
> *opening like a furrow*
> *filling me with a longing to live*
> *to see it free, beautiful,*
> *full of smiles.*
>
> *I want to explode with love . . .*

4

MADAME SOMOZA'S
BATHROOM

It had become the custom, when young writers gathered in the cafés of Managua, to rubbish Ernesto Cardenal. As Father Cardenal was not only the country's most internationally renowned poet, but also the Minister of Culture, I took these attacks to be indications that the country's literature was in reasonably healthy and irreverent shape. The coffee-shop sniping didn't seem to bother Cardenal much. He just went on beaming away, looking, with his little beret and his silver locks and beard, and his *cotona*, the loose peasant's smock he wore over his blue jeans, like a Garry Trudeau cartoon of himself: the radical Latino priest according to *'Doonesbury.'*

The attack that did upset Cardenal, and many Nicaraguans along with him, was the Pope's. The story of Wojtyla's arrival in Managua had passed into legend: Cardenal knelt to kiss the Pontiff's ring, but John Paul II shook angry fists at him and commanded him to regularize his relationship with the Church. The poet burst into tears.

At the time of my visit, neither Ernesto Cardenal nor the

other priest high in the government, the Foreign Minister, Miguel d'Escoto, were permitted to officiate at the Mass. They were, in effect, suspended. As I read Cardenal's poem *The Meaning of Solentiname*, some of the reasons for this rift in the Church became clear:

> *Twelve years ago I went to Solentiname with two*
> *brothers*
>   *in Christ*
> *to found a small contemplative community . . .*
> *contemplation*
> *brought us to the revolution;*
> *and thus it had to be*
> *because in Latin America*
> *a man of contemplation cannot turn his back*
> *on political struggle . . .*
> *What most radicalized us politically were*
> *the Gospels.*
> *At mass, we discussed the Gospels*
> *with the peasants*
> *in the form of a dialogue,*
> *and they began to understand the essence of the*
> *divine*
>   *message:*
> *the heralding of God's kingdom,*
> *Which is: the establishment on earth of a just*
> *society . . .*
> *At first we had preferred to make*
> *a non-violent revolution.*
> *But later we came to understand*
> *that right now, in Nicaragua,*
> *non-violent struggle is not possible . . .*
> *Now everything has come to an end in our*

community.
Solentiname
was like a paradise
but in Nicaragua
paradise is not yet possible.

I met Cardenal in Hope Somoza's bathroom. The Ministry of Culture occupies what used to be the dictator's residence, and the Minister's office, he gleefully informed me, had once witnessed Mme Somoza's daily *toilette.* Had he ever been here, I asked, in the bad old days? No, no, he exclaimed, throwing up his hands in a parody of what would once have been perfectly legitimate terror. 'In those days the place was surrounded by guns, tanks, helicopters. It was frightening just being in the neighbourhood.' I told him of my own experience of being in the neighbourhood of a Somoza, and he was delighted. 'Then you know everything.'

He showed me round. 'This was the bar. That is the Japanese house which Hope Somoza liked to use for her meditating. Here, for the guards, and here, for the horses.' Concrete tennis courts cracked and decayed in the rain. I felt that the re-allocation of this house of barbarity to the Ministry of Culture was a particularly elegant revenge, and so, clearly, did Cardenal.

Back in Hope's bathroom we discussed his development as a poet. There was the early influence of Neruda – 'his lyric mode, not the political stuff' – and, later, the much more profound impact of North America: Pound, Whitman, Marianne Moore. We also talked about the parallel development of his political radicalism. 'In the beginning I was a sort of Christian Democrat. I had many arguments with Carlos Fonseca and the others. I was against the revolutionary route at that time. They were always very patient with me, very gentle.' This, after all, was a man who had entered a Trappist monastery when he was thirty-one. Revolution did not come naturally to such an inward, contemplative spirit.

The turning-point was his visit to Cuba, immediately after the revolution there. 'It was a conversion,' he said. 'When I got back, I announced that I had been converted. It created a great scandal.' He beamed happily at the memory of it.

I said I could understand his conversion easily enough; the Cuban revolution had clearly been a great event for the whole of Latin America, an affirmation of possibility, a demonstration that oppressors could be overthrown. But now, I added, I had serious reservations about Cuba. Did he share any of these reservations? Did he feel, for example, that the Cuban revolution had taken some wrong turnings, and that it could serve, for Nicaragua, as a warning as well as an inspiration?

'No,' he said, with a radiant smile. 'Why? What wrong turnings?'

All right, I thought, he's the Minister of Culture, he doesn't want to find *Cardenal Attacks Cuba* splashed across the world's papers the day after tomorrow. But he was a writer, too . . . I took a deep breath and mentioned, er, for example, human rights abuses? Political prisoners, torture, attacks on homo-sexuals, on, um, *writers*?

'What attacks?'

His serenity threw me into a spin. Confused, I stupidly said, 'Well, for example, on Nicolás Guillén,' who is the head of the Cuban Writers' Union, when I had meant to say, 'Padilla.' He looked at me scornfully. 'In the early days there were a few abuses,' he said. 'But not now.' I asked a few more questions – what about Armando Valladares' book, *Against All Hope*, which speaks of over two decades in Cuban prisons, two decades of being made to eat shit and drink soup containing bits of glass? But it was like hitting a wall.

When I left the Ministry of Culture I noticed that the

Nicaraguan fondness for naming their ministries acronymically had created, in this instance, an unfortunately Orwellian resonance. Cardenal, chief of MINICULT. I went away feeling depressed.

I had lunch with a man from the FSLN's newspaper, *Barricada*. He was responsible for the 'Editorial' page, and I have forgotten his name, which is perhaps just as well, because he made the most chilling remark I heard in Nicaragua. I was arguing with him about censorship in general and the recent closure of *La Prensa* in particular. He seemed, at first, genuinely opposed to censorship – 'of course, as a working journalist, I hate it too' – but then he said this: 'A worker I met recently put it very well. If a mother has a sick child, very sick, she takes it to the hospital without first putting on her make-up.'

My depression deepened. 'So,' I asked unhappily, 'are such matters as the freedom of the press just cosmetic?'

His face lit up, and he nodded enthusiastically. 'Cosmetic, that's the word. Yes.'

'Everybody censors the press in wartime.' That was the official line on the subject, and I heard it from my anonymous *Barricada* friend, from Daniel Ortega, from all quarters. It wouldn't do. I remembered being in Pakistan during the 1965 war with India, and how it felt to be fed information about which the only certain thing was that it was hopelessly and deliberately misleading. I remembered learning to divide Pakistani claims to have shot down Indian planes by ten, and to multiply the admitted losses by the same factor. Then the two figures began to balance up, and you had the illusion of truth. I remembered, too, my outrage at the British government's manipulation of the news media during the Falklands/Malvinas war. What had been unacceptable to me there was also unacceptable here.

The issue of press freedom was the one on which I

absolutely parted company with the Sandinistas. It disturbed me that a government of writers had turned into a government of censors. Largely because of this issue, a kind of silent argument raged in my head throughout my stay. I would tell myself that something remarkable was being attempted here, with minimal resources and under great pressure. The land reforms, and the health and literacy campaigns of 1980 and 1981, the years before the start of US aggression, showed what could be achieved. The literacy campaign, for instance, had brought the percentage of illiterate Nicaraguans down from more than fifty per cent to less than twenty per cent in two years. Now, however, the diversion of manpower into the war effort meant that the initial campaign had not been properly followed up, and illiteracy was creeping forward once again, like a jungle reclaiming a neglected clearing . . . Then I would argue back: those campaigns are all very well; but they think that dissent is cosmetic. And *Barricada* is the worst paper I've seen in a long while.

The argument usually ended in the same place. Nicaragua was an imperfect state. But it was also engaged in a true revolution: in an attempt, that is, to change the structures of society in order to improve the lives of its citizens. And imperfection, even the deep flaw of censorship, did not constitute a justification for being crushed by a super-power's military and economic force.

Mario Vargas Llosa wasn't in Nicaragua, but in the quiet of my room I would dispute with him, too. He had written and spoken so frequently, and with such skill, about the importance of supporting the democratic process in Latin America; he insisted that it was the only way to break the cycle of revolution and dictatorship. He justified his support for parties and governments of the right in his native Peru by saying that he preferred ballots to bullets; that a flawed democracy was infinitely preferable to no democracy at all.

Peru was a flawed democracy of the right. Nicaragua was a flawed democracy of the left. If democracy were really Vargas Llosa's goal, then Nicaragua, according to his own declared principles, was exactly the kind of state he ought to be supporting, and fighting to improve.

I wondered, into the silence, why he did not.

5

ESTELÍ

At five a.m. on the morning of 19 July, the day of the seventh anniversary celebrations, I went to the home of Daniel Ortega and his wife, the poet Rosario Murillo. After getting past the usual compound walls and guards, I entered a rambling bungalow of many verandahs and large numbers of carved wooden rocking-chairs. The decor reflected Rosario Murillo's interest in the country's arts and crafts: there were brightly coloured wooden animal mobiles dangling from the beams, and pottery decorated with pre-Columbian motifs, and cushions covered in the softened bark of trees. The house revealed very little about Comandante Daniel, for whom, it seemed, reticence had become (had always been?) second nature. Children's toys, and indeed children, were everywhere. There was no shortage of little Ortegas, and many of them, I noted, were wearing 'Masters of the Universe' T-shirts, featuring the eternal battle of He-Man and Skeletor; another indication of the omnipresence of US culture.

The Sandinista leadership assembled. This year, the main

'Acta' or celebratory event was to be held at Estelí, the
northern town, just forty kilometres from the Honduran
frontier, that had always been solidly behind the Frente. (Even
the local bishop was the most amenable member of the Nicaraguan church hierarchy.) The decision to hold the Acta at
Estelí was an act of defiance, and it was a racing certainty that
the Contra forces would be doing their best to ruin the day.
'We will show them we can defend our frontier,' Daniel
Ortega said.

Pragmatically, four of the FSLN 'nine' stayed behind in
Managua, as did Sergio Ramírez. We set off in convoy, pre-
ceded by the now-familiar outriders in their orange washing-up
gloves. Their hands, I thought, must get terribly hot and sticky
in there.

The Nicaraguan people knew what to do when the rubber
gloves approached: they got out of the way. We zoomed
northwards. Daniel Ortega drove his own, black Landcruiser.
I travelled behind him with Rosario Murillo and two of
the 'nine', the agriculture minister Jaime Wheelock and the
FSLN's political chief, Bayardo Arce, in Comandante Arce's
vehicle. Arce looked impatient as we bowled along (he has a
reputation for being something of a speed merchant). Scare-
crow Ronald Reagans hung – by the neck – from roadside
trees.

Arce munched on an enormous cigar as we crossed the
bridge at Sébaco. 'It would be a good day,' he remarked
absently, 'for the *contra-revolución* to attack a bridge.'

'Hmm,' I agreed, keeping my voice deep and courageous.
The road was lined with members of the peasant militias in
fatigues, carrying their Kalashnikovs. 'We decided to use the
militias for security purposes today,' Arce said. 'We couldn't
pull the troops in from the frontier, as you'll understand.'

'Hmm,' I agreed again. In Sébaco, I noticed, you could go

and play bingo at the Red Cross building. They obviously didn't get too much work, I reassured myself.

'The security seems excellent,' I mumbled. Jaime Wheelock, baby-faced and friendly, grimaced. 'There are a lot of roads,' he said. 'We can't guarantee that they are all safe.'

'Oh,' I said. 'I see.'

Wheelock was worried that the Contra would hide out along the smaller mountain roads and ambush the *campesinos* as they made their way to Estelí. Many rural communities had been instructed not to try and make the trip into town for the Acta for this reason. 'We are trying to keep it as much of a local event as possible,' Wheelock said. 'In a way it's a tribute to the people of Estelí, who have sacrificed very much.'

The mountains were closing in ahead of us. We were in a heavily cultivated valley, and suddenly Wheelock launched into his favourite subject: agrarian reform. It was extraordinary the way that cherubic countenance would light up the moment the talk got round to pigs or coffee or rice. In this valley, he said, the mixed economy was functioning perfectly. That, over there, was a large private farm, and there were some small private farmers and over there, state-owned farms. The state offered the private sector expert advice, technical assistance and even acted, at peak harvest times, as a supplier of labour.

'The *campesinos* used to be forcibly shunted around the country under Somoza, didn't they?' I asked. 'So how is it that they are so willing to become travelling labourers for the revolution?'

'Obviously we don't make them move by coercion,' Arce spoke, his words sidling past the obstacle of his cigar. 'It requires persuasion, political work.'

Wheelock said, 'It's because we have given them land. Now they have their own land, they have a base. And then different harvests happen at different times, so it is a way for them to use their slack periods profitably.'

'Still, it's surprising they're willing to be so mobile,' I said.

Wheelock smiled happily. 'It is because they have great trust in the revolution, now.'

O the beauty of the mountains at Estelí. They sprang from the earth in improbable, contorted forms, in shapes *plenty of fantasy*, as the old tobacco map had put it. Sixty or seventy thousand of us had crowded into the plaza, cradled by the mountains' encircling arms. Banners waved: *power to the people*. And, on the Tannoy, as we waited for the Acta to get under way, there was 1950s rock music. Estelí danced to *'Rock Around the Clock'*.

Backstage, in a hospitality room under the main stand, the Sandinista leadership was receiving messages from the front. Short-wave radio brought the news that two large Contra groupings had been identified, and had crossed the frontier into Nicaragua. Ortega, Arce, Wheelock and the others went out to greet the crowd.

Daniel Ortega would never be a natural orator, but according to the old hands I asked, he had become much, much better at public speaking than he used to be. 'You should have heard him last year,' one party worker whispered to me. 'Phoo!'

I thought he spoke simply and well, if a little stilted when he waxed rhetorical. He said, not for the first time, that Reagan was 'worse than Hitler', and that was plain silly. But he was much more effective when he listed the numbers of teachers, doctors, volunteer workers and *campesinos* who had died in the last year, and spread his arms wide after each statistic to demand from the people: *'Quién es culpable?'* (Who is to blame?) And they roared back their answer: 'Reagan.'

One day, he said, when Nicaragua was at peace, history would remember there was a nation that would not lie down and be crushed.

'*Patria libre!*'

'*O MORIR.*'

That evening we were back in Managua, and the good news was that the the Contra had not managed to do a single thing all day. No roads had been mined, no *campesinos* attacked, no bridges blown. *Nada*. At the old Somocista country club, Managua was having a party. Salsa and bossa nova music filled the night sky. I looked at the dancers and thought that it was not the moment for an *escritor hindú* to disgrace himself by attempting to compete with such performers.

Somebody took my elbow. I turned to find a small, elderly gentleman with a cane nodding meaningfully at me. He was, of course, a poet. 'I greatly admire,' he said to me, 'your Indian poet, Tagoré.'

I was taken aback. What was old Rabindranath doing here, with this accent on his final e? 'Is he translated here?' I asked.

'Victoria Ocampo, the great Argentine editor and intellectual, fell in love with the work, and with the man,' came the reply. 'I do not know, however, if they had an *affaire*. I suspect not. But Victoria Ocampo was determined that Latin America should discover this great genius, and she published many excellent translations.'

'Then Tagore is better read in Latin America than in India,' I said. 'There, many of the translations are very bad indeed.'

'Tagoré,' he corrected me. 'I admire him for his spiritual qualities, and also his realism.'

'Many people think of Latin America as the home of anti-realism,' I said. He looked disgusted. 'Fantasy?' he cried. 'No, sir. You must not write fantasy. It is the worst thing. Take a tip from your great Tagoré. Realism, realism, that is the only thing.'

I escaped from the admonitory shade of Rabindranath and sat down with Rosario Murillo and Hugo Torres, the Frente's political education chief (and, what else, a poet). Also at the table were Susan Meiselas, the American photographer whose work in Salvador and Nicaragua I had long admired, and an American film producer, Burt Schneider. I arrived as Rosario was wondering how the people of the USA could tolerate what their government was doing to this tiny country.

'You've got to understand that for Americans, Nicaragua has no reality,' said Burt, a tall rawboned man with long arms and large gestures. 'To them it's just another TV show. That's all it is.' He went on to argue that the US would never invade Nicaragua because of the memory of Vietnam. Susan Meiselas said she found it hard to be so optimistic. So did I; in neo-conservative America, the lesson of Vietnam seemed to be that the real mistake had been to quit when they did, instead of staying to finish the job.

'The trouble is, Rosario,' Schneider cried, 'nobody knows if you're communists. Hell, I don't know myself. What do you reckon, Susan?' He leaned conspiratorially across the table to Meiselas, 'Does she look like a Commie to you?' Schneider had known Rosario a long time, and she and Torres both smiled politely, but the joke fell pretty flat.

In the background, the nine *comandantes de la revolución* were having their picture taken. It was the only time I ever saw them all together, and my only glimpse of Tomás Borge, a tiny gnome with a large cigar.

'Look at them,' Burt said lovingly. 'Looks like a school photo, doesn't it? Isn't it a privilege to be here with them, on this day?'

'Yes,' I said, 'it is.' Happy birthday, Nicaragua. I drank a toast in the best rum in the world, Flor de Caña Extra Seco. Mixed with Coke, it was called a Nica-libre, and after a few glasses I was ready to take on the salsa champions and knock them dead. I went outside to dance.

6

THE WORD

In the octagonal church of Santa María de los Ángeles in the Riguero *barrio* of Managua, Father Uriel Molina stood in full regalia in front of a packed congregation with a pop group at his back. The modern church looked like a tepee of metal girders. Its walls were covered in luridly coloured murals. Sandino, wearing his hat even though he was in church, and Carlos Fonseca, his goatee and specs looking iconically, as they always did, up and into the future, were both present on the walls, but on modest side-panels, playing a strictly supporting role, on this occasion, to Christ and his angels.

(The characteristic Fonseca pose was clearly based on the old images of Lenin thrusting his beard forward, ever forward. It struck me that, in this supposed hotbed of Marxism-Leninism, this was as close to a picture of Lenin as I'd come. I did, eventually, get to see both Vladimir Ilyich and the old bastard Marx himself: their portraits flanked a rather bemused-looking Sandino at the headquarters of the biggest trade union, the CST [Central Sandinista de Trabajadores]. Compared to, for example, Kerala, where graffiti of Lenin speaking Malayalam sprouted on every second wall, and trucks could be named STALIN JOSÉ, the Reds in Nicaragua were keeping a pretty low profile.)

I had come out to this poor *barrio*, whose people had been prominent in the insurrection, to hear the 'Misa Campesina', the peasants' mass created by Ernesto Cardenal and Carlos Mejía Godoy, whose gift for the hummable tune might be envied by Paul McCartney. The Misa Campesina was one of the most striking manifestations of liberation theology, which, in Nicaragua, had introduced into church services such versicles-and-responses as: 'Between the Church and the Revolution/There is no contradiction.' I had also wanted to get a look at Father Molina, one of the most visible of the liberation-theology priests, an early influence on Luis Carrión, and the founder of the Valdivieso Centre, at which the ideas of the Popular Church were hammered out. The expelled Bishop Vega had attacked the Valdivieso Centre people as a bunch of liars. 'The problem is that they use the Marxist method. For a Marxist . . . to tell a lie is valid because with it you can better implant the ideology.' And the American journalist Shirley Christian, in her book *Nicaragua: Revolution in the Family*, a book that was waspishly hostile to most aspects of post-Somoza Nicaragua (and, among other things, presented a sympathetic portrait of an escaped Somocista officer of the National Guard, Leo Salazar, who called Somoza 'a wonderful man'), described Father Molina as 'a television talk-show host.'

He was certainly flamboyant, something of a showman, a priest familiar with the hand-held microphone. He led the service with a theatrical jauntiness that had clearly offended Ms Christian. I, however, infidel that I was, quite enjoyed it.

The guitars and drums struck up a tune, and the lead singer sang:

Vos sos el Dios de los pobres,
el Dios humano y sencillo . . .

'You are the God of the poor,
the human and simple God,
the God with the work-hardened face,
that's why I talk to you . . .
just as my people do,
because you are the worker God,
you are the labourer-Christ.'

The tunes of the Misa Campesina were real foot-tappers; the lyrics continued in this quotidian vein. 'Identify yourself with us, O Lord,' they asked at one point, in a revealing reversal – after all, it was more traditionally the role of the faithful to identify themselves with the deity – 'Show us your solidarity.' The God of the Poor had to earn the people's belief, by being one of them.

The texts for the day came from the book of Exodus, and, in his sermon, Father Molina wove them into an extended metaphor, in which the people of Nicaragua were equated with the Israelites in their Egyptian captivity. Somoza was cast as the Pharaoh, and the FSLN was likened to Moses, leading the people across the parted waters of the Red Sea into the Promised Land, while behind them, the God of the Poor closed the waters over the head of Rameses-Tacho and his National Guard.

The idea that a people could be exiled inside their own country, that Nicaragua could be Egypt as well as the land of milk and honey, was a striking and fertile one. But Molina made no mention, I noticed, of the years wandering in the wilderness; no reference to the Golden Calf.

In the congregation was a delegation of farmers from the

American Midwest. No lovers of Reagan themselves, they had come down to learn about Nicaraguan farming methods and give what help and advice they could. There was no shortage of US citizens in Nicaragua; the previous year, for example, a group of Californian old-age pensioners had come down to help bring in the coffee harvest, having heard that the man-power requirements of the army – 50,000 troops stationed along the Honduran border – were making it very difficult for the farmers to get in the crop. (The Nicaraguans had nick-named them the 'grey panthers'.)

For the benefit of the US farmers and the other *brigadistas* (foreign volunteer workers) in the church, Molina led us in a chorus, in English, of *'We shall overcome'*. Like many people who absolutely can't sing, I get sentimental about old tunes; the lump in the throat provides an excuse for the painful fractured noises emerging from the mouth. 'Deep in my heart,' I yelled, threatening the glass in the windows, 'I do believe, we shall overcome some day.'

Whether or not we would, I thought as I left the congrega-tion, being unwilling to participate in the taking of body and blood, one certainly had to believe in the power of this new version of Christianity, and in its popularity. It confirmed what I'd been told by Swedish missionaries, foreign journalists and Nicaraguan friends, and what Dr Conor Cruise O'Brien sug-gested in an essay in the London *Times*: that the divisions in the Church in Latin America had now gone so deep that the Vati-can must be getting nervous. There was a very real possibility of a second Reformation, a second breach with Rome.

At the home of another formidable priest, the Maryknoll father who is now Nicaragua's subtle and erudite Foreign Minister, Miguel d'Escoto, the size of the problem to be overcome was made abundantly clear. D'Escoto reminded me of Friar Tuck, a jolly fat man of considerable toughness. He was in a lot of pain from a slipped disc, but ignored it all evening, even though it was hurting him just to sit. 'I can see the break of diplomatic relations with the US coming very soon,' he said. 'It's even possible that the US may persuade Honduras, Costa Rica and Salvador to break with us as well. They can't get the support of all the states in the region for an invasion, so it seems they want to set up a little mini-group, and then that mini-group can invite them to attack us.' But the Nicaraguans would never be the ones to make the diplomatic break. 'It's our position that a dialogue is essential.' We sat drinking cold water amongst his collection of Nicaraguan art, for which he hoped to find a private sponsor to build a permanent home, a museum. He had offered it to the state, but Daniel Ortega had said that the state already owned too much, it would be better to keep the exhibit out of the government's hands.

We looked out on to a wonderfully kept tropical garden, his other great love. 'I've never said it before,' he said, 'but now I think the Americans will come. The invasion will happen.'

The Misa Campesina was still fresh in my thoughts, so we talked about the Church and the revolution, about the battle taking place for the Word. 'With the priests, there's no problem,' he said. 'Most of them are with us. But the Nicaraguan church hierarchy has always, sadly, been very reactionary, very bound up with the old oligarchy. The Jesuits have no problems, either.' Managua's Jesuit university was flourishing, with plenty of financial backing from the Government. I asked why it was that liberation theology had made so little impact on the Church hierarchy. 'There are plenty of fine minds in the Nicaraguan church,' d'Escoto said. 'Plenty of original thinkers. But none of them have access to Obando y Bravo. The Cardinal is afraid of people with minds. He surrounds himself with persons who have attained the minimum level required for ordination.' And, after a pause: 'The trouble with Obando is that he hasn't read a book since the revolution; and he hadn't read one before it, either.'

Susan Meiselas arrived with Burt Schneider. There had been gunfire in the neighbourhood, probably a few boozy militiamen still celebrating the seventh anniversary. Susan had wanted to investigate, but hadn't done so. This surprised d'Escoto. 'What's this? Is this Susan Meiselas telling me she kept away?' Meiselas had been in the thick of the fighting during the insurrection, after all.

'Well,' she said, 'I had to protect Burt, you see. Who is wearing white, I might add.' Burt looked a little, but not very, abashed.

Susan had recently returned from the Philippines, and had been delighted to discover that in a local park known for its romantic assignations the new Filipino President's name had become a saucy joke: *'Corazón, aquí, no?'* That is: 'Darling, let's do it here, eh?' Or, if the words were stressed differently: *'Corazón, aquí? – No!'* She obviously loved being in Nicaragua. 'This place is ruining me financially,' she said. 'I've got an apartment in New York that I have to pay for, but I spend all my time down here.' She had recently made a documentary about the wealthy Barrios family, a clan divided, like the journalistic Chamorros, by the revolution: an anti-revolutionary patriarch whose sons were all with the Frente. (The two families were connected by marriage: Violeta Chamorro of *La Prensa* was a Barrios by birth. Nicaragua often felt like a village, because one kept stumbling over such connections. Luis Carrión's uncle, to give another example, was Arturo Cruz, banker and opposition presidential candidate.) She seemed reluctant to screen the film in Nicaragua. 'It's not for here,' she said. D'Escoto described a documentary he had made, in which

interviews with affluent Nicaraguan women, who spoke of the
laziness and colour televisions of the poor, were juxtaposed
against footage of the impoverished homes and lifestyles of the
actually existing poor. Susan nodded. Her film was a lot less
polemic, more ambiguous than that. The patriarch had fasci-
nated her. 'I wanted to understand how he could think what he
thinks, knowing what he knows.' It was that ambiguity which,
she felt, might make some Nicaraguan audiences uneasy about
the film. 'But we aren't used,' she said, 'to hearing people speak
without doubt. When you come from here, the situation can
seem very clear-cut, very black and white. But we aren't used
to it.'

D'Escoto described the visit to Managua of a White House
emissary – whom I'll call 'Rocky'. During their talks, he told
us, he himself had repeatedly emphasized that, given goodwill on both sides, he was convinced that the difficulties
between the US and Nicaragua could fairly straightforwardly
be resolved. ' "We understand," I said, "that you have certain
security requirements in this region. That's fine. We can discuss
all those. We are pragmatic people, and we want a working
deal with the United States." '

Eventually (d'Escoto continued), Rocky took up the gaunt-
let. If they were hypothetically to suppose that this hypothetical
goodwill might hypothetically exist, on what basis did the
padre think that negotiations might begin?

'Well,' d'Escoto said (this was before the Hague judgment),
'suppose we both agreed to abide by international law? That
would be a fairly objective basis.'

'That's your problem, Father,' Rocky told him. 'You're a
philosopher. You won't concentrate on the facts.'

And what were the facts? D'Escoto, an excellent raconteur,
performed Rocky's reply. 'These contras on your frontier,

Padre. They give you lots of trouble, don't they?' Yes, d'Escoto had replied, but they wouldn't if you stopped funding them. 'There you go again,' Rocky said. 'More philosophy. You're hopeless, Father. The reality is that these people have been funded, are being funded and will continue to be funded. And they give you trouble. *Those* are facts.' He then said he thought Father Miguel looked pretty intelligent. 'And intelligent men don't want trouble. And you've got trouble.'

So what did he suggest, d'Escoto asked. 'It's easy,' came the reply. 'Just do as we say. Just do as we say, and you'll see how this trouble you've got will disappear. Overnight. As if by magic. It just won't be there any more. You'll be astonished. *Just do as we say.*'

It was a well-told, black-comic tale, and since there was no possibility of getting it corroborated it was clearly one of those stories you could either take or leave. 'The truly remarkable thing,' Father Miguel said, 'was how crude the method was.' For a mind as highly trained in disputation, both theological and diplomatic, as d'Escoto's, the American's crassness, his naked gangsterism, had been almost more offensive than the content of the discussion. *'You're hopeless, Padre,'* d'Escoto repeated, laughing a good deal. *'More philosophy.'*

It occurred to me that if the struggle between the Church hierarchy and the priests could be called a struggle over the Word, then this anecdote represented a parallel, secular struggle between two kinds of discourse, vying for supremacy. Before the evening was out, we would find ourselves involved in a third such combat: press freedom again, the other, inescapable, war of the words.

The actual US Ambassador to Managua, Harry Berghold, was not too bad at all, d'Escoto was saying. He had been put in because he was supposed to be an expert on Marxism-Leninism. (His previous posting had been in Hungary.) 'The trouble is that now he says he can't find any Marxism-Leninism here.' Poor Berghold, his reports on Nicaragua languishing on the desk of the duty officer in Washington, unread by the makers of policy. He was summoned from time to time to the US capital, to give briefings on Marxism-Leninism. 'But at these meetings they never ask him about Nicaragua. It is sad, really.'

At this point, Burt Schneider, who had obviously been bursting with it, unleashed a diatribe against the closure of *La Prensa*. 'It's a stupid mistake,' he said. 'It cancels out the Hague judgment, and it takes away my ability to argue. Now, when people in the US say the Sandinistas are undemocratic, I've got nothing to tell them.'

D'Escoto gave us the party line: all countries have the right to censor the press in wartime; *La Prensa* was being financed by the CIA; it was an important part of the US strategy of opening an internal front, just as they did with the paper *El Mercurio* during the destabilization campaign against the Allende government in Chile. But he seemed to distance himself from the decision at two moments. The first was when he mentioned, mildly, that he had been out of the country when the decision was made, so he had not been present at the crucial Cabinet meeting. The second was when the argument had been raging (or, rather, Burt had) for some time. 'This argument,' Father Miguel said, 'reminds me of Cabinet meetings. We have exactly the same disputes.'

But, he said, while the government was anxious to have a good press abroad, and to help its liberal supporters, there were decisions that had to be taken on national security grounds, and that was that. 'If you want to answer people on the subject of democracy, talk about the Hague ruling. That shows who is acting legally and who is not. By bringing that case we have given you a very powerful argument. Use that.'

Susan Meiselas and I were broadly in agreement with Burt. We said that it felt as though a downward spiral had begun: first the US approved aid to the Contra, so the FSLN closed *La Prensa*, so the *New York Times* called them Stalinists, so they expelled a couple of priests . . . it was like going into a tailspin, and the inevitable smash – a US invasion – got closer and closer each time round. 'You shouldn't get caught in that spiral,' Susan said. 'You shouldn't become so predictable.'

I voiced a rather different fear. 'I've lived in a country, Pakistan, in which the press is censored from the right, by a military regime. And to tell the truth the papers there are better than they are here. But what worries me is that censorship is very seductive. It's so much easier than the alternative. So, no matter what reasons you have right now for closing *La Prensa*, I don't like it. Not because of what you are, but because of what, if this goes on, you might eventually become.'

Father Miguel had his wall up again. 'These are only wartime measures. In peacetime, it would be different.'

Maybe, in the end, it came down to this, I thought as I left Miguel d'Escoto's home: who did I think these people really were, beneath the public positions and military fatigues? Father Miguel, Sergio Ramírez, Daniel Ortega: were these dictators in the making?

I answered myself: no. Emphatically, no. They struck me as men of integrity and great pragmatism, with an astonishing lack of bitterness towards their opponents, past or present. They were revolutionary nationalists, a breed not always despised in the United States, which was also born of a revolution, and not so very long ago, at that.

For the first time in my life, I realized with surprise, I had come across a government I could support, not *faute de mieux*, but because I wanted its efforts (at survival, at building the nation, and at transforming it) to succeed. It was a disorienting realization. I had spent my entire life as a writer in opposition, and had indeed conceived the writer's role as including the function of antagonist to the state. I felt distinctly peculiar about being on the same side as the people in charge, but I couldn't avoid the truth: if I had been a Nicaraguan writer, I would have felt obliged to get behind the Frente Sandinista, and push.

I remained convinced that the FSLN's policy of censorship was misconceived and dangerous. When Omar Cabezas, Nicaragua's chief of political direction at the Ministry of the Interior, and a roguish, piratical figure, gave the New York PEN Congress the party line – censorship would stop when US aggression stopped – I heard a journalist murmur: 'Don't hold your breath.' And at the end of his speech, one of the writers in the hall, an East European writer, not an American, called out: 'That was a policeman's speech.' The FSLN would do well to take notice of such opposition.

But to oppose a government's policy was not to oppose the government. Not for me, anyway; not this government, not yet.

7

⚜

EATING THE EGGS OF LOVE

I first read Omar Cabezas' book, *Fire from the Mountain*, on the
plane from London to Managua. (The English title is much
less evocative, though shorter, than the Spanish, which trans-
lates literally as 'The mountain is something more than a great
expanse of green'. Now, on the road to Matagalpa, travelling
towards the mountains about which he'd written, I dipped into
it again. Even in English, without any of the 'Nica' slang that
had helped make it the most successful book in the new
Nicaragua (its sales were close to 70,000 copies), it was an
enjoyable and evocative memoir of 'Skinny' Cabezas' recruitment by the FSLN, his early work for the Frente in León, and
his journey up into the mountains to become one of the early
guerrillas. Cabezas managed to communicate the terrible difficulty of life in the mountains, which were a hell of mud, jungle
and disease (although one of his fans, a young Nicaraguan sol-
dier, thought he had failed to make it sound bad enough
because he had made it too funny). But for Cabezas the mountains were something more than a great expanse of unpleasant-

5 4

ness. He turned them into a mythic, archetypal force, The Mountain, because during the Somoza period hope lay there. The Mountain was where the Frente guerrillas were; it was the source from which, one day, the revolution would come. And it did.

Nowadays, when the Contra emerged from The Mountain to terrorize the *campesinos*, it must have felt like a violation; like, perhaps, the desecration of a shrine.

Forested mesas flanked the road; ahead, the multiform mountains, conical, twisted, sinuous, closed the horizon. Cattle and dogs shared the road with cars, refusing to acknowledge the supremacy of the automobile. When the trucks came, however, everybody got out of the way fast.

Tall cacti by the roadside. Women in fatigues carried rifles over their shoulders, holding them by the barrels. Moss hung in clumps from the trees and even from the telephone wires. Children pushed wooden wheelbarrows full of wood. And then, as we neared Matagalpa, we came upon a sombre procession carrying a distressingly small box: a child's funeral. I saw three in the next two days.

It had begun to rain.

I was pleased to be getting out of Managua again. Matagalpa felt like a real town, with its church-dominated squares, its town centre. It was like returning to normal, but normality here was of a violent, exceptional type. The buildings were full of bullet-holes left over from the insurrection years, and dominating the town was a high, ugly tower which was all that remained of the National Guard's hated command post. After the revolution, the people had demolished the Guardia's fearsome redoubt.

The ice-cream shop had no ice-cream because of the shortages. In the toy shop the evidence of poverty was everywhere; the best toys on display were primitive 'cars' made out of a couple of bits of wood nailed together and painted, with Coca-Cola bottle tops for hubcaps. There were, interestingly, a number of mixed-business stores known as 'Egyptian shops', boasting such names as 'Armando Mustafa' or 'Manolo Saleh', selling haberdashery, a few clothes, some toiletries, a variety of basic household items – shampoo, buckets, safety-pins, mirrors, balls. I remembered the Street of Turks in *One Hundred Years of Solitude*. In Matagalpa, Macondo did not seem so very far away.

The faces in the Egyptian shops didn't look particularly Egyptian but then neither did the orientally named Moisés Hassan, mayor of Managua. In the cafés, I met some more familiar faces. Posters of the Pope and of Cardinal Obando y Bravo were everywhere, the Cardinal's scarlet robes rendered pale pink by the passage of time. Sandinistas, unconcerned about the company they were keeping, drank hideously sweetened fruit squashes, including the bright purple *pitahaya*, and munched on the glutinous kiwi-like *mamón*, beneath the watching Cardinal. I talked to Carlos Paladino, who worked in the office of the *delegado* or governor of Matagalpa province, about the regional resettlement policy.

Large areas of the mountainous and densely jungled war zone in the north-eastern part of Jinotega province had been evacuated, and the population relocated in southern Jinotega, and Matagalpa province, too. It had been a 'military decision', that is, compulsory. The army had been having trouble fighting the Contra because the scattered civilian population kept getting in the way. The people were also in danger from the Contra, who regularly kidnapped *campesinos*, or forced them to grow food for the counter-revolutionary soldiers, or killed them. But wasn't it also true, I asked, that many people in those areas sympathized with the Contra? Yes, Paladino replied, some men had gone to join them, leaving many women with children behind. The large number of one-parent families of this type had become quite a problem. But in many cases the men would return, disillusioned after a time. The government offered a complete amnesty for any *campesino* who returned in this way. 'We don't hold them responsible,' Paladino said. 'We know how much pressure the Contra can exert.'

Resettlement brought problems. Apart from the single-parent issue – how were these women to be involved in production when they had to look after their children? – the resettled northerners were people who were utterly unfamiliar with living in communities. They had led isolated lives in jungle clearings. Now they were being put into clusters of houses built close together. Their animals strayed into their neighbours' yards. Their children fought. They hated it. Many of them were racially different from the local *mestizos*: they were Amerindians, Miskito or Sumo, with their own languages, their own culture, and they felt colonized. 'We made many mistakes,' Carlos Paladino admitted.

The plan was to have child-care centres at each co-operative settlement, but so far they had only been able to put in eleven such centres in over fifty communities. They had also managed to build some schools, some health-care facilities; but there was still a lot of resentment in the air.

The lack of resources (and, no doubt, the haste with which the operation had been carried out) had meant that in some places the authorities had been unable to provide the resettled families with completed houses. The 'roof only policy', as it was called, offered the uprooted families exactly what its name suggested: a roof. They had to build the walls out of whatever materials they could find. It was not a policy calculated to win hearts and minds. But, Paladino insisted, the state was doing its best, and international volunteer brigades and relief agencies were helping, too. There were even some unexpected individual initiatives. 'A few days after the mine blew up and killed the thirty-two bus passengers,' he told me, 'a tall, fair-haired man appeared in the area, a foreigner, with fifteen hundred dollars to give away. He was just carrying it in his pockets, and looking for the families of the thirty-two, to hand over the money. It was his savings.'

Progress remained slow. 'It isn't easy,' Carlos said. 'Eight new communities have been destroyed by the Contra in the last six months. Hundreds of *campesinos* die in the attacks every year.'

Our best defence is the people in arms. 'The people are more and more able to undertake their own defence. In November 1985 at Santa Rosa hundreds of Contra were killed. Since then, in the attacks on the new co-operatives, hundreds more.'

But the Contra were doing damage, all right. For a country in Nicaragua's position, the loss of an estimated forty per cent of the harvest was a crippling blow.

When Carlos Paladino came to work in Matagalpa, he was highly critical of the way the revolution had handled the resettlements, and won the approval of the regional *delegado*, Carlos Zamora, for his new approach. He went into the jungle, with his staff, and lived with the peasants for months, to learn about their way of life and their needs, before attempting any resettlement. This altered the layout of the new settlements, and greatly increased the officials' sensitivity to the people's wishes. Paladino became an expert on Miskito Indian culture, and had started writing about it. In his spare time (!) he was doing a history degree. Not for the first time, I felt awed by the amount people were willing to take on in Nicaragua.

After I'd been talking to him for more than an hour, I discovered that Paladino had been in hospital twenty-four hours earlier, having a .22 bullet removed from his lung. It had been there since before the 'triumph', the result of an accident: he had been shot in training by a careless cadet. He opened his shirt, after I had bullied him to do so, and showed me the scar. It was an inch away from his heart.

I stayed in a wooden chalet in the mountains high above Matagalpa, and that night the *delegado*, Carlos Zamora, and his deputy, Manuel Salvatierra, dropped by to inspect the *escritor hindú*. Zamora was small, slight, moustachioed; Salvatierra of much bigger build. They were old college friends. We sat down to a dinner of beef in hot pepper sauce, squash with melted cheese, and banana chips.

On the 19th, Zamora volunteered, the Contra had moved a thousand men into Jinotega province. Their plan had been to attack one of the two hydro-electric stations and cut the power cable. They had also intended to ambush *campesinos* on their way to Estelí. 'They failed completely,' he said with satisfaction. 'Our intelligence was good enough. But 700 of them are still in the region, still in Nicaragua. The rest have returned to Honduras.'

Salvatierra stressed the Contra's morale problem. 'They're scared of us,' he said. 'Dollars won't help that.'

I changed the subject. Was it true that it cost six head of cattle to get a car serviced? They laughed. 'Or ten hectares of maize,' said Carlos Zamora. So, then, I said, if prices are that high, tell me about corruption. They looked embarrassed, not unexpectedly, but they didn't refuse to answer. Yes, Zamora said, there was, er, some. 'About the car service,' he said. 'You see, a mechanic will tell you that a certain part is unavailable, or can be ordered for crazy money, but he just happens to have one at home, for a price.'

The black market accounted for maybe forty per cent of the country's liquid assets. 'Anything that can be bought can be sold down the road for more,' Salvatierra said. 'There is an old woman who hitchhikes from Matagalpa to León every day, with a suitcase full of beans, mangoes and rice. She earns 5,000 córdobas a day. I earn about 3,000.'

Zamora and Salvatierra had been 'bad students' in Managua when the FSLN recruited them. Zamora's father was a garage mechanic. (I had accidentally hit on the right subject when I talked about servicing motor cars.) 'He wasn't against the revolution but he wasn't for it, either.' I said that it seemed at times that the revolution had been a struggle between the generations – the Frente's 'muchachos', kids, against the older generation of Somocistas and cautious, conservative campesinos. No, no, they both hastened to correct me. But the impression stuck.

'How old are you?' I asked them. They giggled prettily.

'Thirty,' Carlos Zamora said. He had fought a revolution and was the governor of a province, and he was nine years younger than me.

Later, when a little Flor de Caña Extra Seco had loosened things up, the old stories came out again: of the battle of Pancasán in 1974, at which the Sandinistas suffered a bloody defeat, but after which, for the first time, the campesinos came to the Frente and asked for arms, so that the defeat was a victory, after all, the moment at which the muchachos and the peasants united; of Julio Buitrago; of the local boy, Carlos Fonseca, who was born in Matagalpa. Sandino and Fonseca were both illegitimate, they told me. 'So what's the connection between bastards and revolutions?' I asked, but they only laughed nervously. It wasn't done to joke about the saints.

I tried to get them to open up about the period in the '70s during which the Frente had split into three 'tendencies', after a bitter dispute about the correct path for the revolution. (The 'proletarian faction', led by Jaime Wheelock, believed that a long period of work with the campesinos, to politicize and mobilize them, was the way forward, even if it took years. The faction that favoured a prolonged guerrilla war, and based itself in the mountains, included Carlos Fonseca himself; and the third faction, the *terceristas*, which believed in winning the support of the middle classes and proceeding by a strategy of large-scale urban insurrection, was led by Daniel Ortega and his brother. The factions united, in December 1978, for the final push to victory, and it was the *tercerista* plan that carried the day.)

Zamora and Salvatierra denied that there had been any internal power struggles; the division had been tactical and not a real split. 'I've never heard of a revolution without a power struggle in the leadership,' I said. 'Wasn't it true that Jaime Wheelock was accused of being responsible for the split? Wasn't it true that Daniel Ortega became President because the *tercerista* faction won the internal fight?' No, they said, anxiously. Not at all. 'The directorate has always been very united.'

That simply wasn't true. Where had they spent the insurrection years, I asked; 'In the cities,' Zamora replied; Salvatierra nodded. Now I understood: they belonged to the urban-insurrectionist, *tercerista* faction, the winning team. They didn't want to seem to be gloating over the victory.

To stir things up, I said that the case of Edén Pastora suggested that the divisions were deeper than they cared to admit. After all, Pastora had been a *tercerista* himself, he had been the famous 'Commander Zero', glamorous and dashing, who had led the sensational attack on the Palacio Nacional, taken the entire Somocista Chamber of Deputies hostage, and obtained the release of fifty jailed Sandinistas plus a half-million dollar ransom; and there he was today, in exile in Costa Rica, having tried to lead a counter-revolutionary army of his own . . . He had been defeated by the Sandinistas, but surely his break with the revolution he helped to bring about was significant? There were grins and embarrassed laughs from the *delegado* and his deputy. 'Edén Pastora wanted personal glory,' Salvatierra said. 'He joined the wrong army in the first place.'

The next day I drove up into the north. I knew that the road I was on, the one that went up past Jinotega and headed for Bocay, was the one on which the Contra mine had exploded, killing 'the thirty-two', and even though that had happened a good deal further north than I was going, I felt extremely fearless as we went over the bumps. 'How do you protect the roads?' I asked the army officer who was accompanying me. 'It's impossible to guarantee total safety,' he replied.

'I see,' I said. 'Yes. By the way, how do you know when there's a mine in the road?'

'There's a big bang,' came the straight-faced reply.

My breakfast of rice and beans – 'gallo pinto', it was called, 'painted rooster' – began to crow noisily in my stomach.

There were vultures sitting by the roadsides. Low clouds sat amongst the mountains. The road-signs were punctured by bullet-holes. In the jeep, the driver, Danilo, had a radio, or rather a 'REALISTIC sixteen-band scanner', on which he picked up Contra transmissions. We passed co-operatives with resolutely optimistic names: *La Esperanza. La Paz.* The mountains thickened and closed: walls of tree and cloud. There was a flash of electric-blue wings; then, suddenly, a peasant shack surrounded by trees and hedges clipped into cones, domes, rectangles, spheres, all manner of geometric shapes. To be a topiarist in a jungle, I reflected, was to be a truly stubborn human being.

Then there was a tree lying across the road, blocking our way. Was this it? Was this where Contra fiends with machetes between their teeth would burst from the foliage, and goodbye *escritor hindú*?

It was just a tree across the road.

～❀～

The Enrique Acuña co-operative was named after a local martyr, who had been murdered by a wealthy local landowner after Somoza's fall. (The killer got away, fleeing the country before he could be arrested.) It was a 'CAS', a Cooperativa Agrícola Sandinista, that is, a proper co-op, with all the land held and farmed collectively. Elsewhere, in areas where there had been resistance to the co-operative idea, the government had evolved the 'CCS', the Co-operative of Credits and Services. In a CCS the land was owned and farmed by individuals, and the government's role was limited to supplying them with power, water, health care and distribution facilities. There was no doubt that the *campesinos* were encouraged to adopt the CAS structure, but the existence of the alternative was an indication of the authorities' flexibility; this was not, surely, the way a doctrinaire commune-ist regime would go about its business.

The houses were built on the 'miniskirt' principle: metal roofs stood over walls that were made of concrete up to a height of three feet, and of wood above that height. This had become the *campesinos'* favourite building method. The Contra couldn't set fire to the roofs, or shoot the occupants through the walls while they lay sleeping. The houses were arranged around wide avenues, with plenty of space between them. Pigs were snoozing in the shade. There was a tap with running water, and even a shower. In a ramshackle shed, a playschool was in progress: clapping games and songs. In the next room, there was a baby care centre with instructions for the care and diagnosis of diarrhoea pinned up on the wall, written out and illustrated by the children themselves. The disease was the main child-killer in the rural areas.

All around the co-operative's residential area was a system of trenches. The *campesinos* did guard duty on a rota basis, and many of the men were familiar with the workings of the AK-47 automatic rifle. They were also geniuses with the machete. The *campesino* who had hacked to pieces the tree that had held us up could have shaved you without breaking your skin. Alternatively, he could have sliced you like a loaf.

Last November, the Contra had attacked the Acuña co-operative, by daylight and in force: around 400 of them against thirty-two armed defenders. Arturo, the burly young man who was in charge of the defence committee, told me proudly that they had held out for three hours until help arrived from a neighbouring co-operative. In the end the Contra were beaten off, with thirteen dead and around forty wounded. 'We lost nobody,' Arturo boasted. Since then, the Contra had been seen in the neighbourhood twice, but had not attacked.

A thought occurred to me: if the opposition were correct, and the Sandinistas were so unpopular, how was it that the government could hand out all these guns to the people, and be confident that the weapons would not be turned against them? There wasn't another regime in Central America that would dare to do the same: not Salvador, nor Guatemala, not Honduras, not Costa Rica. While in tyrannical, 'Stalinist' Nicaragua, the government armed the peasantry, and they, in turn, pointed the guns, every one of them, against the counter-revolutionary forces.

Could this mean something?

I got talking to a group of five *campesinos* during their lunch break. They parked their machetes by hacking them into a tree-stump, but brought their AKs along. Did they know anyone who had joined the Contra? They knew of kidnaps, they said. But how about someone who had joined voluntarily? No, they didn't. The people were afraid of the Contra.

One of the *campesinos*, Humberto, a small man with a big-toothed smile, was an *indigène*, but he wasn't sure what sort. He wasn't Miskito or Sumo, he knew that. 'I'm trying to find out what I am.' He had lived in the north, in the area now evacuated. The Contra, he said, had kidnapped him, threatened to kill him, but he had escaped. A while later he heard that they were still after him, and intended to recapture him. 'This time they'd have killed me for sure.' So he was delighted to be resettled. 'It was hard at first, but, for me, it was a blessing.' He sat close to a matchstick-thin man with wiry black hair sticking out sideways from beneath his peaked cap. 'The same happened to me,' this man, Rigoberto, said. 'Just the same story. Me, too.'

Another of the quintet came from a coastal fishing community, where there had been no possibility of getting any land. The other two were locals. 'So do you think of this as your home now?' I asked. 'Or does it seem like just some temporary place?'

Arturo, the defence organiser, answered. 'What do you mean? We've put our sweat into this earth, we've risked our lives for it. We're making our lives here. What do you mean? Of course it's home.'

'It's our first home,' the fisherman, the oldest of the five, at around fifty, said. He was called Horacio, and as I listened to him the penny dropped. What he had said, and what the *indigène* Humberto had told me – 'I'm trying to find out what I am' – were both connected to Father Molina's sermon in Riguero, to the idea that one's own country can be a place of exile, can be Egypt, or Babylon. That, in fact, Somocista Nicaragua had literally *not been* these people's home, and that the revolution had really been an act of migration, for the locals as well as the resettled men. They were inventing their country, and, more than that, themselves. It was by belonging here that Humberto might actually discover what he was.

I said, 'You're lucky.' The idea of home had never stopped being a problem for me. They didn't understand that, though, and why should they? Nobody was shooting at me.

The co-operative's day began at five a.m., when the workers assembled to hear the day's work rota from the representatives of the various (annually elected) committees. Then they went home, breakfasted on tortillas and beans, and were in the fields (coffee, rice) at six, working for around eight hours. After work there were adult education classes. Three of the five men I spoke to had learned to write since arriving here – Humberto, he confessed, 'not very well.' The classes went up to the fourth grade.

What did they do for fun? Cockfighting, cards, guitar music, the occasional social call at the neighbouring co-op, the odd trip into Jinotega or Matagalpa, and of course the various fiestas. But they seemed awkward talking about fun. 'In spite of the men lost to the war effort,' Arturo insisted on getting the conversation back to the serious stuff, 'we have kept up our levels of production.'

With the generosity of the poor, they treated me to a delicacy at lunch. I was given an egg and bean soup, the point being that these eggs were the best-tasting, because they had been fertilized. Such eggs were known as 'the eggs of love'. When people had so little, a fertilized hen's egg became a treat.

As I ate my love-eggs, which really did taste good, there were children playing in the shack next door to the kitchen hut. Their playing-cards were made out of rectangles of paper cut out of an old Uncle Scrooge comic book. *Waak! My money! You dratted* . . . Pieces of Huey, Dewey and Louie fled from the rage of the billionaire American duck. While on a radio, I promise, Bruce Springsteen sang '*Born in the USA*'.

The Germán Pomares field hospital, on the road back to Jinotega, was named after the FSLN leader who had been killed in May 1979, just two months before the 'triumph'. Pomares had been a great influence on Daniel Ortega, and was one of the most popular Sandinista leaders. 'He was so loved,' my interpreter told me, 'that his death wasn't even announced on the news for six months.' I added this to my collection of depressing sentences, alongside the one about the 'cosmetic' nature of press freedom.

At the sentry box at the hospital gate everybody was supposed to hand in their weapons, but our driver, Danilo, hid his pistol under a sweatshirt I'd taken off as the day grew hotter. Stripping in the heat was one thing, but he would have felt underdressed, he agreed when I discovered his deception, without some sort of gun.

The hospital was just two years old. 'We have had to develop it quickly,' said the director, Caldera, an Indian-looking man with a picture of Che, made of tiny shells, hanging on his office wall. 'Never in the history of our nation have we had so many wounded.' The specialist staff were all Cubans. Nicaraguan doctors were gradually being trained to take over, but, at present, simply didn't have the skills required for this kind of surgery.

The average age of the patients was twenty-one. Ten per cent of them were regular soldiers, thirty per cent came from the peasant militias, and no less than sixty per cent were youngsters doing their military service.

'That's astonishing,' I said. 'Why so many military service casualties?' The reason, Caldera said, was that these kids were the main components of the BLI forces, the small commando units that would pursue the Contra deep into the jungle, into The Mountain. Military service in Nicaragua was no joyride.

In recent months, many of the hospital's patients had been mineblast victims, and almost all of these had died. Otherwise the main injuries were from bullet wounds. 'Eighty-three per cent heal completely,' said director Caldera, who knew his statistics. 'Six to seven per cent survive with disabilities.' That left ten per cent. I didn't ask what happened to them.

By chance, I visited the Pomares hospital when there were quite a few empty beds, and very few amputees. Usually, Caldera said, things were different. 'If it was always this way I could write poetry.' Another poet. There was no escape from the fellows.

I asked if they had to import blood. No, he said, the national blood donation programme provided enough. That struck me as fairly remarkable. It was a small country, and it had been losing a lot of blood.

The young men in the wards were all gung-ho, all volubly starry-eyed about the revolution – 'Since my injury,' one teenager told me, 'I love this revolutionary process even more' – and all super-keen to return to the fray. I met a nineteen-year-old youth who had been fighting for six years. I met a shamefaced seventeen-year-old who had shot himself accidentally in the foot. I met an eighteen-year-old with wounds all over his body. 'First I was hit in the leg,' he said, 'but I could keep firing. Then the shrapnel, here,' he indicated his bandaged forehead, 'and my vision blurred. I passed out, but only for a moment.' I asked about the alarming gash above his right knee. 'I don't know,' he said. It looked too large to have arrived without being noticed, but he shook his head. 'It's funny, but I just don't know how I got it.'

They were all very young, yet already so familiar with death that they had lost respect for it. That worried me. Then, as I was leaving, I met a young woman in a wheelchair. She had been shot in the groin, and her face was glassy, expressionless. Unlike the boy soldiers, this was someone who knew she'd been shot, and was upset about it.

'And what do you think about the revolution?' I asked her.

'I've got no time for that junk,' she replied.

'Are you against it?'

'Who cares?' she shrugged. 'Maybe. Yes.'

So there were people for whom the violence was too much, and not worth it. But it also mattered that she had been entirely unafraid. She had been in the presence of several officers of the state, and it hadn't bothered her a bit.

When I was back in my chalet, the mountains looked so peaceful in the evening light that it was hard to believe in the danger they contained. Beauty, in Nicaragua, often contained the beast.

8

ABORTION, ADULTHOOD
AND GOD

The most important task facing the National Assembly was the drafting of the new Nicaraguan constitution. I went along to the Assembly building, which still looked like a bank, to meet four members of the constitutional committee, two of whom, inevitably, turned out to be poets: Luis Rocha and Alejandro Bravo. A third, Manuel Eugarrios, was a journalist, and the fourth, Serafín Soria, was the FSLN's chief whip.

In the general election, the FSLN won sixty-one of the ninety-six seats in the Assembly. The others were divided between six opposition parties, four to the right of the Frente and two tiny ones, the PS and the Marxist-Leninist MAP, to its left. (The left parties regularly attacked the Sandinistas for being fakes, not revolutionaries at all; the Frente leadership seemed to enjoy these attacks.) Initially all the opposition parties co-operated with the constitution committee, but then Dr Virgilio Godoy of the Liberal Party, which was actually to the right of the Conservatives, and held nine seats to the Conservatives' fourteen, refused to participate. 'He wants to keep apart,' Rocha said, 'to make himself an option for the United States.'

(This tendency to dismiss their opponents out of hand could land the Sandinistas in some trouble. After my return, I heard that Godoy had persuaded the other opposition parties to join him in refusing to take part in the constitutional process until the FSLN agreed to discuss the 'great problems' facing the country. Even though, on this occasion, the opposition did not insist that the Contra leaders be party to such talks, it seemed likely that the constitution could become a political football.)

At the time of my visit, the first draft had been completed and then discussed, up and down the country, in seventy-three public forums. Alejandro Bravo said: 'This is the first time in the history of Latin America that the people have been consulted on their constitution.' The draft constitution spoke of 'the construction of a society with broad based participation of the people, the right to vote and to be elected, freedom of speech, organization and assembly, and the rights to housing, education and health care.' It defined political pluralism as 'the participation of all political organizations without ideological restrictions, except to those who advocate a return to a Somoza style of government.' It stipulated 'a mixed economy . . . where diverse forms of property exist – state, private, mixed and co-operative – and where the principal objective is the well-being of the people, without impairing the ability to maintain reasonable profits.'

'Every person,' one clause read, 'has the right to freedom of conscience, of thought, of religion . . . No one can be subject to coercive measures which violate this right.' The State was obligated to provide social security, welfare, and 'protection against hunger'. It was even responsible for 'conserving the environment.'

There had been no shortage of criticism from the public

forums. At the forum of journalists, writers and cultural workers, one speaker demanded that the constitution should 'amplify the concept of public liberties, freedom of expression and information'. Another insisted that it must 'define the State's policy regarding communication'; a third, more ambiguously, that 'there should be no restriction on freedom of expression, especially for parties representing the working class'.

The committee was re-drafting the constitution in the light of all the comments. A two-thirds majority was technically required for each clause, but, Eugarrios said, 'We are trying to work by consensus. We want a pragmatic constitution that will last.'

Wasn't it true, though, that there were a number of issues on which such a consensus would be impossible to form? 'I want,' I said, 'to ask you about abortion, adulthood and God.'

Of all the issues raised in the people's forums, the right to abortion on demand had come up most often. Women all over Nicaragua had demanded that this right be included in what many of them considered a very male constitution. But in a country as deeply rooted in Catholicism as Nicaragua, abortion was always going to be an explosive topic.

'Now if such a right were to be enshrined in a constitution,' I suggested, 'it really would be revolutionary.' The men facing me all looked a little shifty. 'We don't think this is a suitable matter for such a document as a constitution,' Soria said. 'What we propose is that immediately after the constitution is ratified we will introduce a bill legalizing abortion.'

'Surely,' I said, 'it could be argued that a woman's right to jurisdiction over her own body *is* a suitable subject for a constitution? It's never been put in one before, but so what?'

'As I said,' Eugarrios answered, owning up to the real reason, 'consensus is very important.' It was clear that abortion wasn't going to make the revised draft.

The question of adulthood was almost as tricky. 'You must remember,' Soria said, 'that in Nicaragua men have been joining the armed forces, and before that the Frente, and dying in great numbers, at the age of sixteen.' I didn't need reminding. The boys at the Pomares hospital clamored in my head: 'I can't wait to get back to the front line!' – 'I'm going next week!' . . . 'So the argument runs,' Soria went on, 'should they not be considered full adults by the constitution?'

Eugarrios, the oldest of the quartet, wasn't happy about that. 'My own opinion is that they should get the right to vote,' he said. 'But full adulthood at sixteen? With the right to borrow money, and so forth? Many people think it's too young, and I must say I am one of those.'

'Many others, however,' Rocha said, 'believe that the *muchachos* cannot be treated as half-adults in this way. We are still discussing this.'

And so to God. In several of the public forums, including the one with the writers, there had been demands that the constitution should 'invoke the name of God as a Supreme Being'. A passionate debate on the subject was in progress all over the country. Where did the committee stand?

The official FSLN position, they told me, was opposed to the idea of mentioning the name, but this wasn't a 'final' position. Some Sandinistas thought that it wasn't very important either way, so if it made some people happy, why not concede it? On the other hand, a number of Christian participants in the forums had said that merely mentioning the name was neither here nor there; it was more important that the constitution should reflect the Christian love-thy-neighbour spirit.

'The ones who are really pushing for this are the Conservatives,' Alejandro Bravo said. So what was the probable outcome? 'It's still uncertain. Maybe God will be in, maybe not.'

With or without God, sixteen-year-old adults and abortion, the constitution ought to have been ratified by the end of 1986. (The subsequent politicking made this less certain.) It struck me, and I said so, as a uniquely important document. But as long as the state of emergency lasted, the constitution would be little more than a piece of paper; the President would retain most of the power, and a number of civil rights would remain suspended. Critics of Nicaragua would argue that the emergency might never end; that it might, in fact, be the first step towards the establishment of a dictatorship. (My own relationship with the term *Emergency*, formed during Mrs Indira Gandhi's dictatorial years of emergency rule in India in the middle 1970s, was an uncomfortable one.)

But the enthusiasm, the vigour with which Nicaragua had entered into the constitution-making process did not smack of window-dressing or tokenism. The emergency in Nicaragua was not the product of a politician's desire to hang on to power, as it had been in Mrs Gandhi's India, but the inevitable response to acts of aggression from outside the country. This was what Sergio Ramírez had meant when he said that peace would bring more democracy, not less.

I left the Assembly building feeling genuinely angry. At the Enrique Acuña co-operative, and again today, I had seen a people trying hard to construct for themselves a new identity, a new reality, a reality that the external pressure might crush before construction work had even been completed.

Nicaragua's constitution amounted to a Bill of Rights that I wouldn't have minded having on the statute book in Britain. But to hell with all that; to hell with all the dead sixteen-year-olds. Give a dog a bad name and hang him.

9

ON CATHARSIS

I was sitting on a verandah at the ASTC cafeteria, in the company of two young Nicaraguan writers, Mario Martínez and Donaldo Altamirano, and two visiting writers from Eastern Europe: the Bulgarian poet Kalin Donkovy, a slow, silent, heavy man, and one of the secretaries of the Soviet Writers' Union, Vladimir Amlissky, a much more urbane fellow altogether. Conversation wasn't easy. Amlissky and Donkovy had to be translated into Spanish by one interpreter, and that was then rendered into English, for my benefit, by a second intermediary. Nevertheless, I thought, one might as well plunge in. 'What news,' I asked, 'does Comrade Amlissky have about the reported liberalization of censorship in the Soviet Union?' He nodded a number of times. 'Things are better,' he said. 'Now more writers, and, which is more important, a greater number of publishers have the confidence to speak out on social issues. I myself have written on the subject of delinquency.' He also told me about all the prizes he had won.

I thought what he said was very likely true. 'But,' I pressed on, 'what about *Doctor Zhivago*? Can we expect its publication soon?'

'My personal opinion,' Amlissky replied, 'is that this novel of Boris Pasternak, *Doctor Zhivago*, is a poor novel. The Nobel Prize was not given to him for literary reasons.'

'To tell the truth, I'm not too fond of it myself,' I said.

'And it made an absolutely terrible film,' he added.

'Yes,' I said, 'but whatever one thinks of *Zhivago*, it has become symbolic of Soviet censorship, and, anyway, you can't seriously be saying that Pasternak was not a writer of Nobel Prize calibre.'

Amlissky nodded again, many times. 'Yes, I think this novel will probably be published soon,' he said, as if it were a trifling thing. 'And, for his poetry,' he added, reasonably enough, 'I would give him all the prizes in the world.'

What about other writers? 'A number of errors were made,' he said, 'in the case of many of our great writers: Akhmatova, Bulgakov, Pasternak. These are now being rectified. For example, the poet Gumilyov, the husband of Akhmatova. A volume of his verse is now being published.'

No mention of Mandelstam, I noticed; and, after all, the 'error' made in the case of Gumilyov was that he had been executed. It seemed an inadequate word to use.

'Yes,' Amlissky said, 'certain errors.' Something of my views had evidently been lost in translation.

'These days, there's a strange schizophrenia in Russian literature,' I suggested. 'Most of the writers known outside the Soviet Union are unread within it, and vice versa. How does that feel to a writer who is still on the inside?'

He answered by attacking the dissident writers. They had ceased to write literature and become pamphleteers. They were mediocre. 'Even if that were true,' I said, 'and as a matter of fact I don't think it is, not when one thinks of Brodsky, Solzhenitsyn, Sinyavsky, Voinovich – but even if it were, mediocrity is no reason for banning a writer. Third-rate writers get published all over the world, after all.'

'Let me give you my personal view of Solzhenitsyn,' he said. 'I don't care for his writing nowadays. It has been getting worse and worse, and he has become a very right-wing figure, very Reaganite, very illiberal.'

I, too, was critical of many of Solzhenitsyn's pronouncements since his arrival in the West, I said; but surely one had to separate that from his stature as the author of, above all, *The Gulag Archipelago*? 'Let me give you my personal view of this work, *Archipelago Gulag*,' Amlissky offered. 'You must understand that in our great classics we have a tradition of high tragedy, in which many awful things are shown and done, but always in the end there is catharsis, the cleansing of the soul. But in Solzhenitsyn we find no catharsis. This is why I do not care for this work.'

I was about to suggest that the lack of catharsis in Solzhenitsyn's writing might have more to do with Russian history than with his artistic limitations, but at this point I realized that the Nicaraguan writers were puzzled and confused. 'The Soviet Union is a country with many great problems,' Mario Martínez said. 'It is interesting to hear how it is learning from its past errors.'

Later, one of the interpreters asked me a breathtaking question: 'What's a labour camp?'

'What's a labour camp?' I echoed, disbelievingly.

'Oh, I can see what you're trying to say it is,' she said. 'Something like a concentration camp. But are you really saying they have such things in the Soviet Union?'

'Um,' I stumbled, 'well, yes.'

'But how can it be?' she asked in obvious distress. 'The USSR is so helpful to third world countries. How can it be doing things like this?'

There is a kind of innocence abroad in Nicaragua. One of

the problems with the romance of the word 'revolution' is that it can carry with it a sort of blanket approval of all self-professed revolutionary movements. Donaldo Altamirano told me how deeply he felt in solidarity with the Provisional IRA.

Now Kalin Donkovy, who had been ponderously quiet all evening, began to speak, as unstoppably as a steamroller, about the poetry of Bulgaria. 'Our tradition is of martyr poets,' he declared. 'Do you know that the symbol of our writers' union is of the winged horse, Pegasus, with a bullet-hole in his chest? The most successful volume of modern poetry in Bulgaria is an anthology of dead poets. And this is not surprising. When poets suffer with the people, their work improves.'

Martínez and Altamirano responded to this statement with great warmth. The parallels with Nicaragua were obvious. The ghosts of the local martyr-poets walked into the ASTC cafeteria and joined us, the ghost, for example, of Leonel Rugama, who, in the old days at the India Café, used to tell stories about his mad uncle who lived in Macondo, with the Momotombo volcano in the background; who died at the age of twenty; and who believed that the revolution was 'communion with the species'.

That was a fine, romantic sentiment, I said to Rugama's ghost. But nation-building required something more prosaic: the ability to make distinctions, for example, between the PLO and the IRA.

I wondered if Nicaragua's ghosts would permit the living to make such distinctions. On the one hand, the romance of the dead; on the other, the great American fist. It could turn into quite a trap.

10

MARKET DAY

The Argentinian writer Julio Cortázar loved Nicaragua, and came here often. When he was in Managua his favourite places were the markets. He would wander, with Tomás Borge, through the old 'Oriental market' that grew up in the earthquake-ruins of the city centre. They must have made an outlandish couple, Julio the giant and tiny Tomás. Nicaragua returned Cortázar's compliment and loved him, too. The author of the fiendishly esoteric and complicated *Rayuela* ('Hopscotch') had been on first-name terms with many market traders. Now he, too, was dead.

When the big new covered markets like the Mercado Roberto Huembes were constructed, the traders didn't want to leave their sites at the Oriental market. They were afraid their regular customers wouldn't be able to find them in the cavernous new location. Daniel Ortega went to a meeting with the traders and old women yelled at him for hours, We won't move, you can't make us go. But some did, and then more, and now very few remained at the Oriental site.

At the Roberto Huembes market there were giant pink bunnies dangling over my head. These were *piñatas*, children's party pieces. You filled them up with sweets and hung them from the ceiling. Then the children beat them with sticks until they burst in a shower of sweets. Young *mestizo* girls eyed the *piñatas* longingly.

There was a distraction. To the music of drums, the *jigantona*, the giant dancing woman, jigged past, about ten feet tall, her head a wide-eyed mask, her hips wobbling. The children rushed along behind her and so did I. She shimmied past a wall on which satirical cartoons had been pinned: Cardinal Obando y Bravo kneeling at Uncle Sam's feet, begging, Give me your blessing, to which Uncle Sam replied, OK, baby, you are Contra, I am Contra, God is with you. Nobody (except for me) glanced at the cartoons. Everyone followed the dancing giantess, who was a lot more fun.

In different parts of the market you could buy furniture, arts and crafts, shoes, household goods, food, more or less anything that the shortages (and inflation) permitted. Some of the shoes cost more than a month's salary for an office worker. Meat, corn, oil, potatoes, beans were all hard to come by. As a result, as I wandered around it, it wasn't hard to hear complaints. Not surprisingly, the government came in for a lot of stick. The shoppers knew that not all the shortages could be blamed on the war. Recently, 20,000 pounds of beef went bad in the government's meat-packing company because it was stored without refrigeration. Then there had been the 200,000 dead chickens to account for. And of course the prices made people angry. They could hardly afford a bottle of shampoo these days.

Because Nicaragua was fertile, people weren't actually starving. There was always the great profusion of fruits to keep the wolf from the door, and, to my India-trained eyes, the scene at the Roberto Huembes was not a portrait of real, grinding poverty. But that argument, the always-someone-worse-off approach, wasn't a particularly good or useful one. There was real hardship in Managua, and real bitching, too.

Many foreign observers, visiting Roberto Huembes and other markets, had used this moaning as a sign that the people had turned against the Sandinistas. I found things to be rather different. The FSLN was attacked all right, until you asked: What should the government do? Should it talk to the Contra, should it make some accommodation with the US, should it sue for peace? The answers to those questions were in an altogether different tone: no, no, of course they can't do that. The war must go on.

The *jigantona* danced away, down the avenue of the cobblers. I went home and read, later that day, about another mythical being. In an interview with Omar Cabezas, he revealed that, instead of the imaginary friends that some children invented, he had owned, until he was about eighteen, an entirely imaginary dog. Gradually, his friends became fond of the dog, too. They would even borrow it for a couple of days at a time. 'It was a group craziness,' he said, 'that I invented.' Leonel Rugama, the poet, was one of the dog-borrowers. Once Cabezas lent Rugama a book and never got it back. When asked where it was, Rugama replied: 'That sonofabitch dog destroyed it!'

Another dog-borrower was a young revolutionary named Roberto Huembes. Like Rugama, Huembes died during the insurrection years, and was now a covered market. Even the dog was dead. 'One day,' Cabezas explained, 'it was run over by a car.'

11

EL SEÑOR PRESIDENTE

When I arrived at Daniel Ortega's house on the evening of 24 July, Miguel d'Escoto was already there, his back a little less painful than it had been the last time we met. News had just come in of an attack by unnamed assailants on some sort of Contra 'summit' in the heart of the Honduran capital, Tegucigalpa. Some of the FDN leaders were thought to have been injured. 'The attack shows how freely the Contra can move inside Honduras,' d'Escoto said. 'They were meeting in a building very close to the house of the President of Honduras. That couldn't have happened without the government's approval.' Who was responsible for the attack? Father Miguel's face was impossible to read. 'Of course, we are being blamed.'

More guests arrived, until most of the country's leading poets and intellectuals were there: Rocha, whom I'd met at the National Assembly; Silva, who ran a children's hospital; Claudia Chamorro, the Nicaraguan ambassador to Costa Rica. Ernesto Cardenal's beam, beret, smock and jeans turned up. So did Carlos Martínez Rivas, about whom people had been worrying for days. Martínez Rivas, a poet notorious for embarking on mammoth drinking bouts that often put him in hospital, had been hitting the bottle again; so when he turned up sober with Sergio Ramírez, there was a general sense of relief. Martínez Rivas was thought by many to be the most innovative, fresh poet in Nicaragua. 'He hates being translated,' Cardenal told me. 'He thinks translation is a form of assassination.' Martínez Rivas' booming good humour, faintly jowly face and bush-shirt that was a little tight at the buttons reminded me of a favourite (and now dead) uncle.

'There's wine in this soup,' he scolded Rosario Murillo sternly. 'What are you trying to do? Make an alcoholic of me?'

Also present was José Coronel Urtecho, a tall Tatiesque man of gentle bearing, who murmured to me as Martínez Rivas and Cardenal began the verbal sparring that would continue all evening: 'They are the two greatest poets of Latin America.' Coronel's modesty was also great; his own reputation equalled theirs.

Rosario Murillo was telling me about her last trip to New York with Daniel. They had decided to try and make a direct appeal to the American people, who were, as the opinion polls showed, mostly opposed to the Reagan policy in Central America. So she had gone on the Phil Donahue show, and Daniel had been filmed by TV cameras as he jogged in Central Park. 'From that point of view things had gone so well,' she said. 'After Donahue people would wave to me in the street and shout *Viva Nicaragua*.' She had even managed to buttonhole Nancy Reagan at a public function and suggest that maybe the two of them might get together and try and mend some fences. Nancy, mumbling awkwardly, had been steered away by her minders at high speed.

'Then Daniel said he needed new glasses.' Rosario asked

some American friends to arrange for a discreet appointment with an optician, and these (very wealthy) friends had insisted that the new glasses would be their gift to President Ortega. When Daniel and Rosario emerged from the opticians they found, to their dismay, that the press were there after all. The next day, the New York papers splashed the story of how the President of impoverished Nicaragua had spent $3,200 on new spectacles. 'That much money,' Rosario said. 'I never dreamed glasses could cost so much. It's true we bought a few pairs, including sunglasses for the children, because we cannot get such things here, but still! And we hadn't paid a cent, anyway, but they didn't print that.' The scandal of the President's spectacles had left its mark. 'You don't know how careful we have to be when we're there. We have meetings scheduled from before breakfast until late at night, and we never eat out anywhere. Endless Chinese takeaways in the hotel room. And then that business with the glasses, really, it was too bad.'

Daniel Ortega entered, with that odd mixture of confidence and shyness. He sat down next to me – we were arranged in our wooden rocking chairs around a long, low table set out in one of the verandahs – and, without any preamble, began to talk politics. He was going to the Security Council in a couple of days' time, to ask America to abide by the Hague judgment. But an interesting thing had happened. He had been approached by a group of US Catholic prelates who wanted a meeting with him while he was in the States. 'This will be one of our most important meetings. It may be they want to mediate.'

'In the matter of the expulsion of Bishop Vega?' I asked.

'Oh, no,' Ortega said dismissively. 'Vega, he's *Cia*. He is completely with the counter-revolution. He has been saying appalling things, that are simply treason by any standards: openly supporting the Contra aggression.'

'And what about Carballo?' I asked, Carballo being the other expelled priest. Ortega was equally dismissive. 'Carballo was Obando y Bravo's other voice. Only he spoke much less carefully. Obando is, still, more circumspect.'

The conversation moved on to the subject of the remaining Nicaraguan bishops. The trouble with them, Ortega said, was that their attitudes were so parochial, so provincial. 'The best one is Estelí, also the one from Bluefields, Schmitt. The rest . . . We opened discussions with them, you know. We said, we know you feel threatened by us, by the revolution. Tell us what your fears are and let's see if we can work something out. We also said we wanted to consult them on various policy matters before making them public. The law on national service, for example, we would have liked to consult them on that. And on other matters, including military business.' But the bishops had been unwilling or unable, he suggested, to speak at that level. 'You know, one of them would pull out a piece of paper with his little local grievances listed on it, and the next would have his piece of paper, and so on. They all came with their private agendas. We had told them to resolve these things at the regional level. But they can't think nationally.' In his view, the bishops were far from unified. 'They often have no coherent view on an issue. But Obando's statements make it seem as if they do.'

Obando y Bravo's theological education, Ortega said, had been paid for by a Somoza crony, a certain Guerrero, known as 'Dr Quinine' because of his dealings in the drug. Then Somoza gave Obando a house, a bank account and a Mercedes-Benz. (An embarrassing photograph existed of Somoza and Obando having a hug.) 'There was a big fuss about the car, because it was such a blatant thing. Finally he had to give it back, but it took him nine months to do so. Nobody knew about the house and the bank account at the time. We didn't know ourselves until after we came to power and could examine the records. We decided it would be counter-productive to move against Obando. So these things have still not been returned.'

He grinned. 'The funny thing is, he and I are from the same village. I knew about Obando's family from my mother.'

In 1974, the FSLN's fortunes, which had been at a low ebb, were revived by a dramatic coup. On 27 December, Sandinista commandos arrived at a fancy dress party at the home of a Somoza crony, Chema Castillo, and kidnapped a group of ambassadors and senior officials. Somoza was obliged to accept their terms. Sandinista statements were put out on radio and TV, a number of political prisoners were freed and a ransom of $2 million was paid. (The commandos had originally asked for $5 million, but two wasn't bad.) The intermediary between the guerrillas and Somoza was none other than Obando y Bravo. And one of the prisoners freed was Daniel Ortega.

'Obando came with us on the plane to Cuba,' Ortega reminisced. 'I went over to talk to him, to say that our families knew each other and so on. But I formed the impression that he was very frightened. I asked him what the matter was and he finally said, "Do you think Somoza put a bomb on the plane?" It was sad; he was afraid that he would be sacrificed.' Ortega, fresh from jail, had to offer reassurance. 'I told him our people had checked the plane and we didn't think there was a bomb. But after a while he was frightened again. This time he said, "Do you think they will arrest me when we land in Cuba?" It was incredible. I said, "Do you seriously think Fidel is going to put you in jail?" It showed how provincial his thinking was.'

I brought the discussion back to its starting-point. 'What will the US bishops offer you, do you think?'

'They will have their own agenda, that's sure; Vega and so on. But maybe they want to mediate between us and the Vatican.'

'Do you really think the Vatican is ready to make a settlement with you?'

'It's possible. There are indications. In the period in which I was refusing to meet Obando, Sergio visited Rome. Before he left, the papal nuncio here in Managua said it was impossible for the Pope to receive Sergio in the present circumstances. But in spite of that, the Pope did receive Sergio, and they had a constructive meeting.' This was fascinating. Perhaps the Pope really had understood how great the challenge to his authority had grown in Central America, and had decided that the God of the Poor had to be placated, made peace with, because he could not be destroyed.

I asked about the forthcoming trip to the UN. 'Presumably the US will use its veto in the Security Council.'

'That's certain,' Ortega agreed. 'But then we can go to the full General Assembly and argue it out there.'

Would Nicaragua be suing the US for damages in the US courts, as had been suggested? 'At this time,' Ortega said carefully, 'we don't want to assume the US has rejected the Hague ruling. We must give them the chance to accept.'

There was an interruption: a quarrel between the assembled great poets. Carlos Martínez Rivas burst into an attack on Ernesto Cardenal's nationwide poetry workshop scheme, under which ordinary people – Cardenal was particularly fond of pointing to the large numbers of participating policemen – could write and discuss poetry. Cardenal was evidently rather proud of the workshops (I had heard him, three years earlier, extolling their virtues at a literary congress in Finland), but Martínez Rivas did not mince words. 'Poetry has stagnated in Nicaragua,' he boomed. 'Nobody reads any more. They only open *Ventana* (the literary supplement of *Barricada*) when they've got something in it. And then they only read their own poems. Anyway, with these workshops, everybody has started sounding exactly the same. Nobody's trying new things, nobody's looking for a new language.'

Having seen some of the workshops' output, I had some sympathy with Martínez Rivas' argument, but kept out of the fight. Cardenal's smile remained in place, but its temperature seemed to have dropped. There was old business between these two. They had been quarrelling for years. They conducted themselves very well, never ceasing to be amicable, to crack jokes, but the dispute was real for all that. From the sidelines, Sergio Ramírez mischievously egged them on, trying to draw Coronel into the fray, but he wouldn't be tempted. Martínez Rivas began to tease Cardenal for being so prolific. 'I remember once, years ago, I was asked to write a poem in two weeks for some fiesta. The winner got to choose the festival queen. I said, how can I write a poem in two weeks? Go ask Cardenal. So they did, and he had something already written that he adapted, and he won the prize. I said, how can you use a thing written in one spirit for a completely different purpose? But anyway, he won. So I said that since I'd arranged it all for him, he had to let me choose the queen. He got the prize, but I chose the girl.'

Amidst these barbed tales of old Managua, I remembered another instance in which Cardenal had adapted an old poem to a new purpose. He had drafted a poem about the death of Sandino, and the fact that his grave was unknown. Then, in 1954, an attempt to capture Anastasio Somoza García, the then dictator, ended in failure. One of the conspirators, Pablo de Leal, had his tongue cut out before being killed. It is said that another, Adolfo Báez Bone, was castrated. The main torturer was Anastasio Somoza Debayle, who would be the last dictator of the line. When Cardenal heard the news, he decided to make Báez Bone the subject of his poem instead of Sandino:

Epitaph for the Tomb of Adolfo Báez Bone
They killed you and didn't say where they buried
your body,
but since then the entire country has been your
tomb,
and in every inch of Nicaragua where your body
isn't buried,
you were reborn.

They thought they'd killed you with their order of
Fire!
They thought they'd buried you
and all they had done was to bury a seed.

When the guests had departed and the dust had settled, I asked Daniel Ortega a few more questions. First, though, he wanted to give me his views on *La Prensa*. 'They can do anything they like, but they must not advocate support for Reagan and the Contra. That's the mark. They went over it. What could we do? Put them on trial? That would have created too much negative attention. So all we could do was close the paper.'

I said: 'I want to be clear about this. I've been told that the problem with *La Prensa* was CIA funding and control. But now you're saying it was the editorial line.'

Ortega replied: 'There's a war on. In peacetime, if *La Prensa* wants to take CIA money, which it did, and push the US line, that's fine. If it wants to attack the Frente, that's also fine. But now it's different. The enemy uses the paper.' The internal front argument again. The fear of a repetition of Chile. Amongst all Nicaragua's phantoms, I thought, there were two darker spectres. Edén Pastora, the skeleton in the cupboard; and Salvador Allende, who was possibly the most important political figure in Nicaragua, after Sandino, anyway.

I asked: 'I've heard many people saying they think a US invasion is inevitable. What's your view?'

Ortega: 'There is a certain fatalism here about this. The situation at the frontier is very tense. Many things could trigger an invasion. For example, in March, we crossed over the Honduras frontier to attack Contra camps. The Honduras government knew we were there, they knew why, they said nothing. It was OK. But the US made a great fuss, moving their personnel and weaponry to the front at a time when we were already falling back. Finally the Honduras government did send us a protest, because of the intense US pressure on them to do so. Now the situation is worse than it was then, because soon, US advisers will be legally allowed to be present by the Congress. So if we shoot down a helicopter and a US citizen dies, it could be provocation. Actually, in March, a US citizen was killed, but since he was there illegally – illegally according to the Congress – Reagan couldn't make anything out of it.

'On the seventh anniversary we deliberately held the Acta at Estelí, to show our determination. After we repelled the two Contra forces that had massed on the frontier, the Honduras government was afraid that, as in March, we would go after them across the border, in "hot pursuit". They actually contacted us to warn us that the US had decided that if we did, that was it, they would attack us. It was very clear. So it could happen at any time.'

I asked: 'Now that the US is spending so heavily to "buy off" your neighbours, do you agree that you are gradually becoming isolated?'

Ortega: 'It's not so easy for the US to isolate us. The people of Central America know that a war here would spread, would become a Central American war. The US had been trying to persuade Honduras, Costa Rica and Salvador to break with us, as you know, and they may succeed. But even Costa Rica, in spite of everything, still has reservations.'

I asked: 'Who was responsible for the attack on the Contra in Tegucigalpa today?'

Ortega: 'We think some guerrillas may have done it. But that fifty Contra leaders could meet so near the President's house: this has disturbed the people of Honduras.'

I asked: 'On the economy: considering the great pressure it's under, how close is it to total collapse?'

Ortega: 'In this special situation, war, we believe that the idea of collapse is not appropriate. You must understand that our people have never been used to great affluence, and minimum subsistence levels are being maintained. We are even slowly improving our agrarian and industrial base.'

I asked: 'But with inflation at 500 per cent, a more or less total strike of investment capital, and a fiscal deficit that represents forty per cent of government spending, are you really saying you can survive indefinitely?' The latest economic indicators were pretty terrible: figures released by the Economic Commission on Latin America showed a three per cent drop in gross domestic product, a five per cent fall in production in manufacturing industry, a vast trade gap. Cotton production had been badly hit by disease and weather and had fallen by nineteen per cent. Low world prices, as well as drought, had meant a reduced income from coffee, sugar and cotton exports (most of the coffee crop had been sold in advance, at 1985 rates, and had therefore missed out on the rise in coffee prices in 1986.)

Ortega gave a somewhat sheepish laugh. 'Well, we have managed so far, and let's say we hope to go on. We subsidize the price of a number of essential commodities, basic grains, oil, soap, beans, agricultural tools. All in limited quantities, of course. The rest of the prices, we have to let them rise, and they have gone up enormously. But at subsistence level the inflation is controlled.'

I asked: 'You make a great deal, understandably enough, of the Hague judgment. But many Western commentators play it down, setting the *La Prensa* closure and the expulsion of the priests against it, "balancing" it, so to speak. How can you hope to win the argument when, rightly or wrongly, the Western media simply don't see the Hague rulings the way you do, and don't give it the column-inches?'

Ortega replied: 'We know there is a lot of sympathy for our case among the people of the United States and Europe. We have to continue to take our case to the people.' More televised jogging, more chat-show politics. The twentieth century was a strange place.

It was one o'clock in the morning; time to leave. As I said goodbye to Rosario Murillo, she seemed already to be bracing herself for the Chinese takeaways of Manhattan. 'The one thing I always look forward to in New York,' she said bravely, 'is the yoghurt.'

'Really?'

'Oh, yes. The wonderful yoghurt. It's the only thing I miss.'

'Enjoy it,' I said, and wished them both good luck in New York. On the way out, I murmured to Rosario: 'And don't visit any opticians.'

After leaving, I was struck by the fact that, throughout the dinner, I had not seen Daniel Ortega actually eat anything. I had been right next to him, and he had turned away all the evening's delicacies, even the turtle meat. (Which had been unexpectedly dense and rich, like a cross between beef and venison. The turtles, incidentally, were protected during the whole of their breeding season, and could only be caught in limited quantities for a few months of the year.)

I found out that he was known for this little habit, which could have been a sign of nervousness, or, more likely, an attempt to make himself seem a man apart, different from the crowd.

And perhaps, when nobody was looking, *el señor Presidente* would sneak into his kitchens and stuff himself in secret.

Map of Bluefields

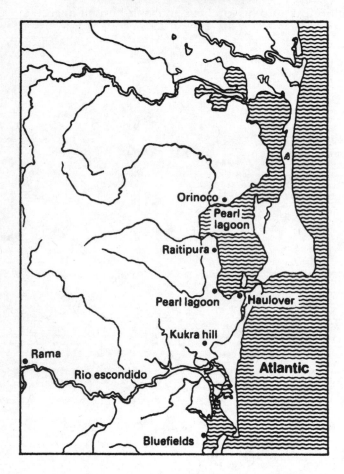

12

THE OTHER SIDE

Rub me belly skin (O mama)
Rub me belly skin (O baby)
Rub me belly skin
With castor oil . . .

The music of Rundown, a local group, played at top volume on a ghetto blaster, welcomed me to Bluefields, on Nicaragua's Atlantic coast. *Costeña* music, Nicaragua's answer to calypso, reggae and ska, had been one of the main reasons why I'd become so determined to get over to Nicaragua's other side. I had also formed an ambition to swim in the Caribbean – because the Atlantic coast was, of course, really the Caribbean coast, as the locals were quick to point out – and the Pacific on the same trip. I'd already had my swim in the Pacific, strolling into the warm, warm water at Pochomil beach near Managua, where once the Somoza gang would take its weekend dips; now for the *Mar Caribe*.

In Bluefields it was often difficult to remember I was still in Nicaragua. The west coast was, for the most part, racially homogeneous, but here, as well as *mestizos*, there were Creoles, three different Amerindian tribes, and even a small community of Garifonos who shouldn't have been there at all, according to the textbooks, but up in Belize. And that wasn't the only difference. The majority of the inhabitants here were not Catholic, but belonged to the Moravian church. And a large proportion of them were English-speaking, to boot.

The culture of Bluefields felt distinctly West Indian, but it was more or less totally cut off from contact with the rest of the Caribbean – excepting Cuba. It wasn't very closely in touch with the Pacific coast of Nicaragua itself, come to that. In Bluefields you couldn't receive Nicaragua's 'Sandinista Television', so you watched the Costa Rican programmes instead. It could take you all day to get a phone connection to Managua, and even then you might not manage it. There was no road link between the coasts. The few air flights filled up weeks in advance, and the only other route involved travelling 100 kilometres on a slow ferry down the Río Escondido (the 'Hidden River' that used to shelter pirate ships in the Days of Yore) as far as the township of Rama, where the 300-kilometre road from Managua came to an abrupt halt. The ferries had been frequent targets for the Contra. About a month before my visit they had burned the penultimate boat. The banks of the river were thickly jungled, and the ferries were sitting ducks; but the people, having no option, continued to use the route.

What would happen when the Contra burned the last boat? The only answer I ever got to this question was a fatalistic shrug. To live in Bluefields was to accept remoteness, just as it was also to accept rain. It was one of the wettest places I had ever been in. 'May is sunny,' people said, but that was cold comfort in July.

⊰⊱

Apart from music and swimming, I was taken to Bluefields by a desire to find out if the revolution still felt, over there, like a new sort of conqueror. The inhabitants of the vast Atlantic coast province of Zelaya (only about 200,000 of them in almost half the country's land area, almost all of it covered with virgin jungle and criss-crossed by inland waterways) had not had much to do with the making of the revolution. As a matter of fact, throughout the country's history, the two coasts had not had much to do with one another at all. The Pacific coast had been a Spanish colony, but even though Columbus had landed in 1502 on the spot where Bluefields now stood, it had been the British who established, in 1625, the Protectorate of Mesquitía. Their subjects were mainly Amerindians: the Mosquitos or Miskitos, the Sumos and the Ramas. The British set up a puppet Miskito 'kingdom'. These Miskito 'monarchs', often educated in the British West Indies or even in Britain, were based in the village of Pearl Lagoon to the north of present-day Bluefields. The Miskitos repressed the Sumos and Ramas so thoroughly that, today, barely a thousand Ramas (and not many more Sumos) were still alive. When I heard this, I realized that my mental picture of the Miskitos as a 'pure' tribal people whose ancient way of life had been disrupted by the Sandinistas, might need a little revision.

Under the British, the Atlantic coast gradually acquired its sizeable Creole population. This was made up in part of runaway slaves from elsewhere in the Caribbean, and in part of people imported by the British to work for them as overseers and clerical staff. Thus, unusually, the British, who were more accustomed to using blacks as slaves, turned them, in Nicaragua, into a petit-bourgeoisie.

The Spanish-speaking *mestizo* population was growing, too, and in 1838 the Republic of Nicaragua was established. *Mestizo* numbers continued to increase, and at the last count they made up over half the population of Zelaya. (The blacks or Creoles, at 50,000 plus, accounted for about a quarter.) Old resentments between the Creoles and the 'pañas' – from *españoles*, Spaniards – had diminished, but the divisions were still occasionally noticeable. The army on the Atlantic coast was almost wholly *mestizo*. This racial division between soldiers and civilians hit me the moment I arrived at the long wooden hut that was Bluefields' airport terminal. The Creoles didn't like joining the *paña* army, though they didn't mind signing on with the police.

The Somoza dynasty handed the Atlantic coast over to the transnational companies, who dug fortunes out of its gold mines and profited also from the abundance of precious woods. The transnationals created, in Zelaya, a distorted, totally dependent company–store economy, habituated to imported US produce and at the mercy of the foreign employers. They exported the area's wealth, put back little or nothing, and when the last Somoza fell they decamped. The effect on the locals' way of life was shattering. And then the Sandinistas arrived, singing heroic songs of revolution and liberty. It wasn't surprising they got a frosty welcome; the revolution of the Pacific-coast *pañas* had felt, to many people on the other side, more like annihilation.

Bluefields was poor as mud. (Only dry places could be dirt poor.) It was too poor to build a waterfront. A few jetties, all loose planks and holes, stuck out into the bay. The wooden houses with their verandahs and balconies looked attractive, but when you got close you saw the rot, the poverty. Children played hoop; Creole ladies lounged on barrels, ample-bottomed and well buttoned-up. *Vote for Yazmina & Fátima*, the walls insisted. I went into a bar in which a *mestizo* sailor, Pancho, was holding forth. 'I've been everywhere,'

Pancho stated. 'Miami. Mobile, Alabama. I've been all over. Let me tell you something: I liked Mobile, Alabama better than Miami, Florida. People don't bother you in Mobile. It's like here, in Bluefields.' The rain began to belt down and Dylan started to sing '*Stuck Inside of Mobile*' in my head. 'Is there any beer?' I asked, and the small jelly of a woman who ran the bar said, 'No. Beer finish.' But when she left the room, Pancho winked and fished out a bottle of *cerveza Victoria* from the cold box. 'Be my guest.'

The proprietress returned and blew her stack. 'Where you find that? Pancho, you no good. These days you got to look after your reg'lar customers, and those beers is reserve. They is reserve. I need meat and ting, I gotta keep the butcher his beer. You got beer at your house, you get me one.' Pancho made mollifying, insincere noises. I felt bad, and didn't enjoy the drink.

After dark, in a Creole bar in the Old Bank *barrio*, I was befriended by Francisco Campbell. He was home on leave from the Nicaraguan embassy in Washington, and he was a man with a problem: the US authorities had just expelled his wife, Miriam, who had also worked at the embassy. He was a likeable, generous man, and put his troubles aside to show me a good time. We ate the bar's special 'chop suey', with which no Chinese person would ever have felt the slightest affinity, but which tasted spicy and delicious, and drank Flor de Caña Extra Seco with tamarind water.

The transnationals, Francisco told me, had been the ones who cut Bluefields' trade links with the Caribbean. He was keen to restore them. 'Do you know Trinidad imports all its beef from Argentina?' he demanded. 'Do you know how many thousands of miles further that is?' He was also eloquent on the subject of shrimps. They spawned in the Escondido tideway and then, in the rainy season when the rainwater pushed the salty water back, they headed out to sea. The lagoon at the river's mouth would fill with shrimps; it would be alive with shrimps. They were the easiest catch in the world. But trawling was banned, because then you'd catch too many, and ruin things for the future. 'Shrimp fishermen from Jamaica have been raiding our continental shelf for as long as I can remember,' he expostulated. 'It's about time we came to some arrangement about that.'

We emerged from the bar when the Extra Seco was gone, and strolled down the street past the Moravian school. The night sky was full of stars, but if you kept looking up at them you were in serious danger of falling down one of the many holes in the road. Francisco had been thinking about his wife, and as we passed the school he cried: 'I was expelled myself once, you know. Right here, from this school.'

'How did it happen?'

'It was the long hair of Mary Hebbert,' he said. 'That did it.' Mary Hebbert had the most beautiful long fair hair, and the young Francisco wanted desperately to attract her attention. One day as he was coming to class – he was not yet ten years old – he saw the hair of Mary Hebbert dangling out of the classroom window. He had an impulse he could not resist: he pulled it. Unfortunately, he pulled too hard, and she banged her head against the window frame. She decided to make a big song and dance about Francisco's bid to be noticed, and the headmaster asked his parents to remove their boy from the school.

'That's terrible,' I said.

'It was OK,' Francisco grinned. 'You survive expulsions.'

'What happened to Mary Hebbert?' I wanted to know.

'I found out,' he said contentedly. 'She married a klutz and lives in the Caymans. So she got hers in the end.'

❧

Cathy Gee, a US citizen working with a local development agency, was telling me about the death of the Rama language when I noticed the smashed computer VDU in her office. The screen had gone, and the insides were in a terrible mess. 'Oh, yeah,' she said. 'Yeah, it was on the boat the Contra attacked. It got shot.' She pointed to something taped to the top of the unit. 'We found the bullet, too. Yeah.' The computer had been a keenly anticipated gift. 'Too bad.'

'So the Contra are assassinating machines now,' I said.

We got back to the Rama language. There were only twenty-three people alive who could still speak it: the other Ramas had already lost their tongue. A French linguist had spent months with the ageing twenty-three, to record the structure and phonetics of the language before it disappeared. 'She came up against quite a problem,' Cathy told me. 'Most of the old Ramas had lost their teeth, so they couldn't pronounce some of the words properly. Yeah.' False teeth were much too expensive to be an option. Dental costs could therefore deliver the final blow to a tiny, dying language. Nicaragua is a land of small tragedies as well as large ones.

Thomas Gordon, the Creole *delegado* of Zelaya's Special Zone II, which included Bluefields, was in his thirties, bespectacled, goateed, and owned a pet macaw. (An English-speaker, he had had to take Spanish lessons, but was by now thoroughly bilingual.) His deputy, Felix, was a *mestizo*, and had the happiest smile I saw in Nicaragua. Originally Felix had been the boss, and Gordon his assistant, but now that the roles were reversed, Felix showed no trace of resentment. The two men bubbled with plans for the improvement of Bluefields. 'This town doesn't even have a decent cinema,' Thomas Gordon exclaimed. 'There are places, but the picture is so dim you can hardly see it. We'll change that. And we're rebuilding the

roads. You may have noticed there are a lot of holes.' I said I
had. 'I'm afraid your hotel is not so good. I want some decent
hotels here. You'll have to come back one May for the Mayo
Ya, and see all the changes.' The Mayo Ya was the music festival that filled the town for one month, with the spirit of car-
nival. I discovered, to my disappointment, that for the rest of
the year the best *costeña* musicians were to be found living in
Managua, and the only way of hearing the music in Bluefields
was on records and tapes.

'You're lucky tonight,' Gordon said. 'We're having a party
for the Cuban doctors. It's gonna be something, man. We're
gonna dance. I mean, we're gonna have a *time*.'

'I'd love to come,' I said. He offered to drive me around
town, and as we drove he soliloquized about the latest employ-
ment projects. 'At Kukra Hill, on Pearl Lagoon, we've got
what could be the oldest working sugar mill anywhere. We had
no funds to modernize it, but recently we found in the jungle a
plantation of precious woods.' A government order permitted
the revenues from non-traditional exports to be retained in the
exporting region (all other funds had to be centrally collected),
so Gordon hoped this one-off sale of rare woods would finance
the renewing of the sugar mill. 'We're gonna get that mill.
We're starting on the operation now, even before Autonomy
comes.'

'Autonomy' was the autonomy project, the biggest political
news on the coast, the scheme that had begun to convince
some Zelayans that their best hopes did indeed lie with the
revolution. I was keen to talk about it, but Thomas Gordon
was pointing out the sights of the town. In Old Bank, the
Creole *barrio*, the wooden houses ranged from sprawling bun-
galows to cramped, spartan shacks. In Central there was a pink
obelisk bearing a white silhouette of Sandino. In Cottontree,
Gordon took me to see his childhood home. 'You know, I've

got a white brother,' he said. 'Tall, pale skin, fair hair, blue
eyes. But he thinks black. I mean, he identifies himself with the
blacks here. That's what counts.'

He introduced me to the macaw, who accompanied us into
the warren of bare-floored wooden rooms, with comfortable
old armchairs and a big airy kitchen. I loved it. Out back was a
large 'yard', a wild garden in which mangoes and breadfruit
hung from tall, spreading old trees. 'How wonderful still to
have contact with the house in which you grew up,' I told
him, a little enviously. He smiled happily. 'I came back to
Bluefields after the triumph,' he said. 'I wanted to do something for my own place.'

I was going up to Pearl Lagoon the next day. 'See the sugar
mill,' he insisted. Also at Kukra Hill there was the new African
palm project. The palms would provide oil, copra, jobs. 'But
they're having trouble getting labour. They should have
known. Blacks don't care to work in plantations any more.'
They: another hint of the old Creole-*paña* friction? He denied
it. 'Before the revolution, it's true, there was some, but that
was in the old society.' Class, racism, sexism, were all deemed
to have been abolished by the revolution. There was something
rather endearing about the idea.

The autonomy project was the FSLN's way of recognizing that
they had made a series of disastrous, alienating mistakes on the
Atlantic coast. Inexperienced, over-zealous young political
cadres had arrived among the Creoles and the Indians and created a good deal of bad feeling, for instance by making all
manner of promises, of new hospitals, schools, and so forth,
promises that the government quickly discovered it couldn't
deliver, because of the war, the scarcities and the inaccessibility
of the region. The arrest of a Miskito leader, Steadman Fagoth,
increased resentment. The FSLN insisted that it had cast-iron

evidence that Fagoth had been a Somoza agent, but the *costeños* weren't interested. Fagoth (who always denied the charges against him) was released, and went instantly into the Contra war. The bridge-building organization known as MISURA-SATA (for Miskitos, Sumos, Ramas and Sandinistas) fell apart after the Fagoth affair and the compulsory resettlement of many Miskitos living along the Río Coco, which formed the frontier with Honduras. Fagoth, dropping the SATA, named his counter-revolutionary force MISURA. In Zelaya, the Sandinistas faced at least four Contra groupings: the main FDN forces; MISURA, still fighting even though the latest word was that Fagoth was no longer its driving force; KISAN, an Amerindian group that had just announced it would use sabotage and speedboat ambushes to try and cut the government's links with sea and river posts on the Atlantic coast; and the Costa Rica-based ARDE forces in the south.

There was no question that the FSLN had seriously mishandled the Miskitos, and attempts to claim that they had heard there was to be heavy CIA bombing in the Río Coco area, and that the evacuations were for the people's safety, only increased the feeling of a cover-up. The autonomy project was an attempt to prove that the Frente had learned from its mistakes. The policy of evacuating Miskitos from the Río Coco had been reversed, and many of them were going back to their old territories. (Some, however, chose not to, having grown accustomed to their new lives.) The policy of unconditional amnesty for anyone returning from the Contra was also having an effect. As morale slumped in the Contra armies, Miskitos were returning to the fold.

The autonomy scheme guaranteed the cultural rights of all minority communities in Zelaya. But it was attempting to do more than simply compensate for previous blunders. Under the scheme, Zelaya would be given a large measure of self-government. The structure of the nation would be altered into a form of federation between the two 'wings', with Managua retaining responsibility for defence, internal security, foreign policy and overall budgetary and economic strategy. Most other functions would pass to a regional executive and a regional assembly. I asked John, a rangy, electric young Creole working at the project offices in Bluefields, if the local administration could actually cope with the new responsibilities. 'In many ways we aren't prepared,' he admitted. 'But we are just going to have to get on and begin it, and learn as we go.'

As I wandered around the cafeterias of Bluefields, I tried to bring up the subject of autonomy as much as possible. The responses I got ranged from suspicion – believe it when you see it – via indifference, to enthusiasm.

The point about the enthusiasm is that there was quite a bit of it, and that it represented the first enthusiasm the revolution had ever managed to generate on the Atlantic coast. 'We never did have a say in our own lives,' one Creole told me. 'First the British ran us, then Somoza and the transnationals. Now, for the first time, we going to get that say.'

When the project was first mooted, many Managuan politicians had opposed it, thinking it smacked of Balkanisation, of the beginning of the break-up of the country. The counter-argument, which had carried the day, was that the project was not dividing the country but recognizing the division that actually existed. By giving the Atlantic coast this degree of independence, the chances were that the bonds between the coasts would actually be strengthened. That paradoxical assessment was borne out by what I saw.

'Autonomy' had even become a hit song for one of the coast's leading bands.

The party for the Cubans in the Bluefields hotel that evening was ostensibly an 'Acta' in commemoration of the storming of the Moncada barracks by Fidel's boys long ago. A young

Creole disc-jockey sat with fierce pride by his sound system, polishing each LP before putting it on, caressing his graphic equalizer like a lover. Bluefields in its party best sat around the walls, reminding me of nothing so much as the school 'socials' I used to go to as a boy in Bombay, all wallflowers and nothing in the middle. The Cubans and Nicaraguans mixed without any sign of difficulty. Six years ago, in September 1980, there had been a Creole demonstration against the Cubans, and relations had been strained. Now, as the DJ put on 'Guantanamera' and the people began to get off their seats and get to work on the dance floor, all that strain had vanished. The Cuban doctors, who had gone without complaint into the most remote regions of Zelaya, regions into which few Nicaraguan doctors had proved willing to venture, had won the locals over. There were still jokes about Cuban accents, but they were friendly jokes.

'Guantanamera, guajira guantanamera . . .' A powerfully built old black woman in thick dark-lensed spectacles, her hair up in a fat netted bun, and wearing a shapeless, white-collared black dress, came on to the floor. Her dancing was so magical, so loose-limbed, so original, that within minutes all the coolest young men in the room were queueing up to partner her. I remembered that one of the traditional Mayo Ya dances was called, and danced by, The Three Old Ladies. The grannies of Bluefields could certainly get down and boogie.

At the party I met a young American health worker, known in Bluefields as 'Mary Carol' because people couldn't get their mouths round her last name, which was Ellsberg. She was married to Julio Martínez, who was in charge of agricultural development in the region; her father was Daniel Ellsberg, of the Pentagon Papers. She had spent a long time working in the villages around Pearl Lagoon – Haulover, Raitipura, Orinoco. When I said I planned to go out there the next day she offered to come and show me round. She had even read, and enjoyed, my novels. It was turning out to be a great party.

The African palm project at Kukra Hill turned out to be Julio's brainchild. He spoke about it with a parent's pride, describing how the rows of saplings had been coming along year after year. I mentioned Thomas Gordon's reservations about the project, and he pooh-poohed the idea that there was a labour shortage. 'The project is going very well,' he said. 'Very well.' He was a softly spoken, scrupulous man, patently dedicated to his work. At his office, early the next morning, he introduced me to Juan Mercado, a Miskito Indian and the first Miskito to become the manager of the Kukra Hill sugar mill. The two of them were off to Managua on business, and apologized for not being able to come along on my trip. 'But Mary will show you everything,' Julio said. As I left, I noticed a poem chalked up on a blackboard at the back of the room:

> *LA REVOLUCIÓN*
> *Se lleva en el corazón*
> *para morir por ella,*
> *y no en los labios*
> *para vivir de ella . . .*

The revolution/is carried in the heart/that it may be died for,/and not on the lips,/that it may be lived by.

Death was here, too. Death, the close friend. It was your child, your mother, your self. It was the invisible object that blotted out the world.

'You haven't been to Bluefields if you haven't had a proper drenching,' Mary said to me as the rain came down in sheets.

'Can we still go to the lagoon?' I asked. She nodded. 'We'll go. Round here it rains so much that, once you've made your plans, you just go ahead with them, otherwise you'd never do anything.'

I had been offered the use of the 'fastest speedboat in Blue-fields'. I climbed aboard with Mary and two Creole friends: Francisco Campbell's sister Yolanda, who ran women's groups, and Edwin, who had brought along an AK-47 that Yolanda was sure he didn't know how to use. As the boat gathered speed the downpour became a pin-cushion stabbing into my face. We zoomed down the forested Escondido and into the swamp-channels between the river and Pearl Lagoon. 'If your boat breaks down on the Escondido, or up in the interior, you're in real trouble,' Mary yelled. 'It can take days, even weeks, before help comes. If it comes.' She had been stranded for three days once.

The thick green walls closed around us. The rain, smashing into our faces, couldn't stop this being a beautiful place; but it did its best.

The township at Kukra Hill wasn't beautiful, though it could boast a new hospital. I waded briefly through thick red mud to have a look at the famous sugar mill. This mill had originally been on the Pacific coast. When its owners considered it obsolete, they dismantled it and packed it off to the other side, where it had gone on running for years, without hope of spare parts, thanks to the improvisatory genius of the local mechanics. As I inspected this museum piece, which looked like something out of the first Industrial Revolution, I found myself fervently hoping that Thomas Gordon's scheme for selling the plantation of precious woods worked out, and soon.

The village of Pearl Lagoon, where once the Miskito kings held sway, and which sits on the shore of the eponymous *laguna* (which never did contain any *perlas*), looked like an idyllic, sleepy sort of place. The well spaced houses were set around three grassy causeways, known as Front Street, Middle Street and Back Street. The two ends of the town had names, too: Uptown, Downtown. Since the revolution they had been renamed according to the calendar-obsessed fashion of revolutions, but if you asked anybody the way to '19 July Barrio' they would look blank, and then, after some moments, exclaim: 'Oh, you mean *Downtown?*'

Three Sandinista soldiers, looking out of place in this Creole settlement, lounged around a little old cannon outside the FSLN offices, whose walls proclaimed, in two-foot red-and-black lettering: *Autonomy now!* Round the corner, on the wall of the school playground, there was an attractively painted mural showing the whole lagoon, with all the villages marked. Hands extended from each village and clasped each other in the centre of the lagoon. 'Bushman,' the legend read, 'surrender is your only salvation.' The bushman being addressed was, of course, the Contra fighter.

The rain had stopped. A thin, jaunty old lady sauntered toothlessly by with her parasol. Yolanda led us to the home of Miss Maggie, the village's great cook. We passed the village meeting-place, which was closed for want of beer. 'Never mind,' Yolanda said. 'Miss Maggie's always got stuff hidden away some place.'

At Miss Maggie's I ate the tastiest meal I had in Nicaragua, once Yolanda had coaxed her into making us something. It was snoek in a hot chilli sauce, and there was even some beer. Miss Maggie, a small, plump, giggling lady with grey hair, also baked sensational coconut bread.

After eating we went to visit Mary Ellsberg's friend, the local midwife, Miss Pancha. She was rocking on her porch in the village's downtown section, and when she saw us approach she let out a whoop. 'Oh, Miss Mary,' she said. 'I was worry when I see you comin' 'cause I did not have my brassiere on. These days I only puts it on when I has company and you done take me by surprise.' Miss Pancha had the largest breasts I had seen in my life, and, Mary told me later, you couldn't actually tell the difference when the bra was on. I was saying hello to Miss Pancha when her pet cow strolled out of the living room and joined us on the porch. 'Say "hi" to my darling, too,' Miss Pancha said.

My visit to Miss Pancha reminded me, finally, that all was not well in Pearl Lagoon, no matter how drowsily jolly the place might seem. The old midwife, laid up these days with back trouble, became melancholy all of a sudden.

'Brought most of this village into the world,' she said. 'Buried plenty, too.'

Round the corner from Miss Pancha's was the house of a young couple who were selling up and moving to Bluefields because the Contra had killed the man's father. In almost every house you could hear a tale of death. Even one of the local Moravian priests had been killed. In a nearby village, the Contra had recently kidnapped more than two dozen children, many of them girls aged between ten and fourteen, 'for the use of the Contra fighters,' Mary told me. One girl had escaped and got home. The villagers had heard that five other children had escaped, but had been lost in the jungle. That was five weeks ago, and they had to be presumed dead. 'It's so sad going there now,' Mary said. 'The whole village just cries all the time.'

On the day of the seventh anniversary, when I was in Estelí, a helicopter crashed in the north of special zone II, killing everyone on board. Mary's husband Julio had intended to be on the flight; it was only at the last moment that other business prevented him from going. The Contra had claimed to have shot the helicopter down, but they hadn't; it was an accident. 'All that fuss about the Challenger space shuttle,' Mary said. 'And how many people died? Seven?' Many of the helicopter dead were from a remote community, Tortuguera. 'The teacher, the army commander, the doctor. Just about all the professionals in the community,' Mary said. 'That place is getting a reputation for being jinxed. That's the third doctor they've lost in a year.' It was Contra policy to kill the professionals when they attacked such communities, but on this occasion fate had lent them a hand. 'In a small society like ours,' Mary said, 'each death is really noticed. You can imagine what a hole twenty-four deaths make. They had the last funeral yesterday. It was a week before they could cut the body out of the wreck and give it to the family. Special divers had to come from Managua to do it. He was a young man, on his way to Bluefields to be married.'

We left Pearl Lagoon and started back to Bluefields. The rain, right on cue, bucketed down again. I decided I no longer needed to swim in the Caribbean. Enough of it had fallen on me from the skies.

Mary Ellsberg came to Bluefields as a *brigadista*, a volunteer worker, thinking she would stay for a year. Instead, she fell in love with the country, and with Julio, and now she was a Nica mother with a one-year-old child, Julito. She was afraid her son might one day have to fight in the war. She had already become enough of a Nicaraguan to think of the war as a long-term, near-permanent reality.

I was surprised to discover an Indian connection. Her father had known and admired the great Gandhian leader, Jayaprakash Narayan, who had led the opposition to Mrs Gandhi during the Emergency, in spite of needing regular kidney dialysis; also Vinoba Bhave, the ascetic philosopher whose life had been spent persuading Indians to give land to the poor. 'My father has been down here three times,' she said. 'The first time, he saw only Comandantes. The second time was really just a vacation. But the third time he was in Bluefields just four days after the Contra attacked. That changed his perceptions pretty radically.' She was still astonished by the naivety of US reactions to Nicaragua. 'When I go back, I show people my slides, and they just say, we had no idea, we had no idea.'

In the speedboat, she and Yolanda talked about childbirth. The real nightmare was having a child in Managua, Mary said. Expectant mothers often had to double up on beds. It was not uncommon for women in labour, and already five centimetres dilated, to be roaming around town trying to get a hospital to admit them. Things were a little better in Bluefields, Yolanda said, and Mary agreed. But when she went into labour her doctor had been at a party. She rang him, but he didn't take the call seriously enough to leave. He rolled up at the hospital the next morning, nursing a hangover when she was already nursing Julito.

'The attitude to pain here is to take absolutely no notice of it,' she said. 'I felt there was a lot of pressure on me not to cry out or moan. I lay there silently, being a sport. Just once, when the contractions were really bad, I let out a noise, and at once one of the women in the other beds said, 'Oh, come on, Mary, it's not as bad as all that.'

Childbirth in Nicaragua was all 'natural' – there simply weren't any drugs to be had – but the women were given no training in breathing or pushing, they did no exercises. Those were things Mary was trying to change with her health care programmes.

Yolanda wanted Mary to come and address a women's

group. OK, Mary said, she was just coming to the end of working with a group of Miskito women.

'These women want first-aid know-how,' Yolanda said. 'Very basic things. How to survive and feed children during and after a Contra attack.'

I asked, tamely, how it felt to live with the constant possibility of dying. Some of the remote regions people like Mary, Julio and Yolanda visited could take sixteen or seventeen hours to reach in a small boat on narrow waterways through dense jungle. How did it feel?

'You learn to live with it. If it happens, it happens,' Mary said. 'People here have come to expect death. The country's youth is just being thrown away.'

Julio was training local people to take over his job, and in a year or so he and Mary might be leaving Bluefields. I thought: I hope you make it. But I didn't say it, or tell her how much I had found, that day, to admire. Instead, I agreed to go to her place the next day, Sunday, and cook her an Indian meal.

On Sunday morning the sun shone. I sat on the porch of my hotel and watched the people hanging out in the street. Across the way was the Instituto de Belleza Ilse, closed today, and there was Ilse on the balcony above her Instituto, sipping her morning coffee. The sun shone, too, on a hump-shaped wooden library building full of Reader's Digest condensed books. In this building, until a couple of months ago, June Beer, librarian, primitivist painter and character of Bluefields, had held sway. Sadly, she had just died.

Church music and reggae passed by on shouldered ghetto blasters. A bright yellow bus bore the sign: 'Passengers not allowed on board with fishes'. The Moravian church rang its bell. Grown-ups and children headed for Sunday school. Second-hand clothes hung, for sale, over wooden verandah railings. Mothers took their children for juice in the town's cafés. At nine the rain poured down; at nine-twenty the sky was blue again. Creole men slapped palms in the street. 'Hey man I hear a tale 'bout you.' It was a moment of peace, and I treasured it. Soon it would be time to go over to Mary's place and cook.

The meal wasn't a great success, because I had never in my life laid eyes on half the vegetables I was preparing; but it was an offering, it was something I could do. Afterwards I said goodbye to Mary and little Julito and headed off down the road. I had a plane to catch.

I met Carlos Rigby, another town 'character', while waiting for my car to the airport. Rigby was a dreadlocked black poet, bilingual in English and Spanish. Dreadlocked but not, I ought to say, Rastafarian.

We talked about his work. These days, he said, he thought it was more important to write in Spanish than in English, although he still did both. 'I am trying to improve my Spanish,' he told me, 'in the vocabularial aspect.' What about his English, I was interested to know: did he, like so many Afro-Caribbean British poets, feel that he ought to write in Creole, in what the Barbadian poet Braithwaite had named 'nation language'?

'Yes, this is a question,' he said. 'But, you know, I come to find writing in Creole a little bit folkloristic.' I said I knew some writers in South London who could give him an argument.

'South London?' he asked, perking up. 'Lambeth? You know Lambeth?'

'I know it,' I said.

'We are twinned with Lambeth,' he said, not without pride.

He then soliloquized for some time about his acquaintance with Ginsberg, who had read and liked a chapter of Rigby's work-in-progress, a fantasy novel of Nicaragua. (Fantasy? What would Tagoré have thought?) He recited a rude poem he had written in Spanish about Obando and Bishop Vega, and carefully explained all the puns. He digressed to tell me about the local witchdoctors, the *sukié*, whom most of the villagers around the lagoon trusted. 'Real witchdoctors,' he promised. 'They dance while prescribing their medicines.'

When the first Western-style doctors had gone into the villages, the people had rejected them, saying they already had their medicine men. Now the government worked with and through the *sukié*. It was another sign of the revolution's adaptability, of its pragmatism.

It started to rain as my car arrived. Rigby said goodbye. 'Soon it going to rain less,' he said. 'In the old days, if Somoza told the rain to stop, it stopped. I don't know what wrong with these Sandinistas.'

Large numbers of black butterflies, black with white spots on the wingtips, were fluttering at the roadsides. Children were swiping at them with sticks. On the airstrip the wind got up and blew a great cloud of the butterflies directly at me. As I walked to the aeroplane the swarm surrounded me, escorting me out of town. It felt like a small miracle; an epiphany.

I reached Managua an hour after the passing of a hurricane that had uprooted trees. It was a good thing the light aircraft I'd flown in hadn't been caught in the storm. Maybe the butterflies had brought me luck.

13

DOÑA VIOLETA'S VERSION

Back in Managua, I had one more ghost to meet. In 1978, when Somoza's growing greed had alienated large sections of the Nicaraguan oligarchy, the editor of *La Prensa*, Pedro Joaquín Chamorro, had started looking like a possible replacement. Somoza had him assassinated, and by doing so sealed his own fate; after that, everyone, even the US, wanted him removed. Chamorro's ghost, shaking its gory locks, appeared at the tyrant's feast and sat down in his chair.

I went to the offices of *La Prensa* to meet Violeta Barrios de Chamorro, Pedro Joaquín's formidable widow, matriarch of the deeply divided Chamorro clan. Her elder son, Pedro Joaquín junior, was in exile in Costa Rica; her younger son, Carlos Fernando Chamorro, was the editor of the Sandinista daily *Barricada*. Of her late husband's brothers, one, Jaime Chamorro, was director of *La Prensa*; the other, Xavier Chamorro, was the publisher of *El Nuevo Diario*, the paper set up by the large group of disaffected journalists who resigned from *La Prensa* after the revolution, claiming that its editorial line had become too conservative. One of her daughters, Cristiana, worked at *La Prensa* (she came in to shake hands during my talk with her mother); the other, Claudia, was the Sandinista ambassador to Costa Rica whom I'd met at Daniel Ortega's house.

Doña Violeta herself was wholly undivided. Her opposition to the FSLN was without shadows or grey areas. 'This is a communist state,' she said. 'The government says we're *Cia*, we're the Reaganite paper. That's OK. Under Somoza we were told we were yellow journalists, we were communists. But we have always stood for peace and democracy. Our leader on the day we were closed down was headed, *We are for peace*. These are the beliefs for which my husband Pedro Joaquín Chamorro was assassinated. They will always be our beliefs. We are not the communists here.'

The first thing I noticed about Doña Violeta was that she wore a great deal of jewellery: gold bracelets and earrings, and quantities of black coral. I had grown unaccustomed, in Nicaragua, to such display, so it struck me in a way it wouldn't have done in London or New York, or even Bombay. There were no concessions being made, the jewellery announced, to the spirit of the 'new Nicaragua'.

The second thing was the frequency with which she would refer to her late husband. It put me in mind of a much younger woman in very different circumstances: Pakistan's Benazir Bhutto, who, knowing that the source of her mass appeal was a ghost, referred to her dead father in every public speech. (She called him *Shaheed sahib*, Mr Martyr.) The martyred Pedro Joaquín had been respected right across the political spectrum, and Doña Violeta was making sure that he was not hijacked by her opponents.

She was a poised, slender woman, very elegant, with short grey hair. Her voice was a fighter's voice: tough, unrelaxed, premeditated. Our interview proceeded down familiar lines. 'In the last four and a half years,' she said, 'we have been more heavily censored than in all the Somoza decades. Thus we see, and the world sees, that the government is taking off its mask, and revealing itself as a Marxist-Leninist, totalitarian state.' The term *Marxist-Leninist*, in Doña Violeta's mouth, was a final condemnation, a judgment from which there was no appeal. 'The TV and radio are state controlled,' she said. 'This paper was the only thing left, and now it has been taken away.' I queried her assertion about the radio – there were, were there not, numbers of independent local radio stations? And wasn't I right in thinking that there was no pre-censorship of the air-waves? – but she swept on. I was handed a dossier of documents relating to the closure of the paper. As she took me through them, she did a rather peculiar thing.

One of the documents was a photocopy of the announcement, published in *Barricada*, of the 'indefinite suspension' of her newspaper. She had underlined two lines near the bottom for my attention. They read:

'. . . esta Dirección resolvió suspender por tiempo indefinido las ediciones del diario La Prensa.'

That is: 'this Directorate has resolved to suspend for an indefinite period the publication of the daily *La Prensa*'. Doña Violeta drew my attention to the words 'this Directorate'. As I knew, she said, the nine-man supreme body of the FSLN was known as the 'National Directorate'. 'So this proves that the decision to close us down was not taken by the government, but by the party.' It was one of her themes: in Marxist-Leninist Nicaragua, the party was the only real power.

As the document was in Spanish, I didn't examine it closely until after the interview. Then I found that it was clearly headed: 'The Directorate of Communications Media of the

Ministry of the Interior'. The same legend was to be found, in display type, at the foot of the announcement. It was obvious that the words Doña Violeta had underlined referred to *this* directorate, and not to the FSLN nine; that, in fact, the document she had handed me proved the exact opposite of what she said it proved.

Doña Violeta also complained, several times, that the Nicaraguan government was the only body with the resources to 'travel everywhere, make any propaganda they want, to tell the whole world their version of what is happening here.' Yet during our interview she mentioned at least two very recent speaking tours of her own, one to Portugal and the other to the United States, 'where I addressed many US Congressmen of all parties on the subject of *La Prensa* and the life of my husband, Pedro Joaquín Chamorro.' And where was the editor of the paper at present? He was abroad. Anyone who read the Western press knew that international journalists beat a daily path to the doors of *La Prensa*, the conservative businessmen's association COSEP, and such opposition politicians as the Liberal, Virgilio Godoy, not to mention Cardinal Obando y Bravo. The idea that the Nicaraguan state could control world opinion – Doña Violeta's poor-little-me ploy – was a second piece of transparent disingenuousness. 'They can say anything they like about us,' she protested, 'and we never have a chance to put our case.' 'You're putting it to me,' I pointed out, 'just as you do to everyone else who comes here.' She gave me her most patrician look. 'I hope, Mr Rushdie, you will not misrepresent what I am telling you.'

'I'll try my hardest not to,' I promised her.

'I want to explain,' Doña Violeta said, 'that Daniel Ortega is not a true president, a president by popular support. The elections were not fair.'

I said that most foreign observers had agreed that they were the fairest ever seen in Latin America, and that surely the fact of an eighty per cent poll indicated that the people had, in fact, given both the elections and the President their backing?

She replied: 'That's what they say, but it's not true. The poll was not so high.'

'How high was it?'

'I don't have the figures right now.'

When we returned to the issue of the paper's closure, Doña Violeta had powerful points to make. I asked: 'I've heard it said, often, that one reason for the closure was that you would publish alarmist stories, about the shortages, for example.' She replied, 'They censor everything. I've told you, four and a half years of censorship. So we can publish nothing that has not been authorized.' It was her best argument: when censorship was already so severe, why close the paper?

'The government says that in time of war your editorial line is unacceptable, that you support the counter-revolution,' I said. She repeated, unanswerably: 'Everything we printed was passed by the censor's office. We would send our articles along with "filler" articles as well, which we would have to use if they turned down our copy. No blank spaces were permitted; no photographs of Hollywood screen goddesses.

'Sometimes,' Doña Violeta added, 'there would be things that the people needed to know. We would print them – we published in the afternoons, and *Nuevo Diario* and *Barricada* come out in the mornings – and we would be censored. Then, the next morning, the same stories would be in the other papers. They had not been censored. We would protest, and then we might be allowed to publish, but it was too late then, obviously.'

I asked: 'Do you have examples of stories that the other

papers were permitted to publish, while your versions were censored?'

'No,' she replied. 'Not at the moment.'

I asked: 'How can you say that the paper is the same as it always used to be, when three-quarters of your journalists quit and started up a rival daily?'

'Oh,' she said, 'they were all Marxist-Leninists. At *La Prensa* we always follow the line of my late husband, Pedro Joaquín Chamorro.'

'But if these were the journalists who wrote the paper in the time of Pedro Joaquín Chamorro, and if they resigned when the paper was under a new editorship, doesn't that mean that the paper can no longer be what it was in your husband's time?'

'Journalists,' she said. 'They come and go. It is like when somebody dies, there is always someone else to take his place. It changes nothing.'

She had referred a few times to an offer worth 'many million dollars' which, she claimed, had been made by Xavier Chamorro of *El Nuevo Diario* to *La Prensa*'s Jaime Chamorro. 'They wanted to buy the paper. So, you see? Several months ago, they had already had the idea to close us down.'

But surely that was not the only interpretation? Perhaps *La Prensa*'s former employees had wanted to regain control over the country's most prestigious title? Doña Violeta remained adamant. She insisted that the offer proved that the FSLN (which did not own *El Nuevo Diario*, although it did put money into it) had been plotting for a long time to shut her paper down.

I said: 'The government claims to have proof that you have taken CIA money, Heritage Foundation money.' 'Let them produce it,' she challenged. 'We have not. But the Marxist government takes money from the Soviet Union and Cuba. And the only people who are truly dedicated to real democracy, they close down.'

Doña Violeta had been a member of the junta that had ruled Nicaragua between the fall of Somoza and the general elections. (The other members had been Alfonso Robelo, the big businessman, now in exile and political leader of the Costa Rica-based ARDE counter-revolutionaries; Moisés Hassan, the 'Egyptian' mayor of Managua; Daniel Ortega and Sergio Ramírez.) She resigned her seat after just nine months, because 'they were not interested in my views. When I agreed to be in the junta it was not for personal gain or anything like that. It was out of a true desire to help build a democracy here. But I soon saw that things were already controlled from outside . . . it was not the authentic thing.'

'From outside?' I asked. 'Could you give some examples?'

'Easily,' she said. 'After nine months I knew we were not fulfilling the oath of office I had taken.'

'But some examples?'

'The advisers who came were Cubans,' she said.

'What made you resign, though?' I asked. 'Was there some issue, some last straw, something you really couldn't stand for?'

'It was for my conscience,' she said. 'They wanted the memory of my husband, Pedro Joaquín Chamorro, and the prestige of this paper, to legitimize the junta. It was meant to be democratic, pluralist. But I quickly saw that wasn't true.'

'But,' I asked one last time, 'what was it that proved that to you?'

'Anyone who comes to Nicaragua can see,' she said. 'You must understand that the majority of our people are true Catholics, not like these religious people who try to divide the Church. The people of Nicaragua who are not Marxist-

Leninist are very sad. That is why we have this war of Nicaraguan against Nicaraguan.'

What was her solution, I wondered. 'The situation in Nicaragua should be resolved without the intervention of Soviets, Cubans or North Americans,' she answered. 'But nothing will be resolved in this country, no matter how many hundreds of millions of dollars are spent, until Daniel Ortega learns to talk to the people.'

I agreed with Violeta de Chamorro that the closure of *La Prensa* was wrong. Apart from anything else, it was evident from the banned articles pinned up by the front door that, because it challenged and argued, it had been the best paper in town. (Not much of an accolade, considering the anodyne nature of the competition.) But her treatment of me did not indicate a profound respect for the truth. She seemed to have no objection to a little helpful massaging of the facts. Also, oddly, she had been the hardest person, of all the people I spoke to, to pin down to specifics. It was usually the politicians' way to make large general allegations unsupported by actual facts and cases. Strange, then, to find a journalist who was so airy about producing hard evidence when requested to do so.

I left with her injunction not to misrepresent her ringing in my ears. I have tried not to do so. But the truth is that I found the idea that this aristocratic lady was closer to the people than the likes of, oh, Carlos Paladino in Matagalpa, or Mary Ellsberg in Bluefields, or even Daniel Ortega, very unconvincing. And I'm practically certain that my scepticism had nothing to do with the jewellery.

14

MISS NICARAGUA AND
THE JAGUAR

My last night in Nicaragua was warm and starlit. I spent it at the home of Tulita and Sergio Ramírez, talking mostly about literature. I heard that *La Prensa*'s 'pope of letters,' Pablo Antonio Cuadra, the one major Nicaraguan poet to be against the revolution, was to have a volume of his work published by the State-run New Nicaraguan Editions; books were not subject to censorship of any kind. (They sold in large quantities, too; print runs of 10,000 regularly sold out. In Britain, with a population twenty times the size of Nicaragua's, most authors would envy such figures.)

In the time of Somoza, there had not been a single publishing house in the whole of Nicaragua. The only way for Nicaraguan writers to get into print was to find a publisher elsewhere in the Spanish-speaking world and then have the books brought in, if possible. It was another reminder of the extent to which things had improved since the time of the Beast, the forty-six years of fear.

The original title of Sergio Ramírez's marvellous novel, *¿Te* *dio miedo la sangre?*, meant 'Were you scared of the blood?' and came from a children's nursery rhyme ('Did your mother kill the pig? Were you scared of the blood?'). The English title, *To Bury Our Fathers*, derived from *The Birds* by Aristophanes:

> The skylark was born before all beings and before the earth itself. Its father died of illness when the earth did not yet exist. He remained unburied for five days, until the skylark, ingenious of necessity, buried its father in its own head.

The novel had been my companion as I travelled around Nicaragua. It was set in the Sandino years, and told a large number of inter-connected stories, which were woven in and out of each other with great skill: the stories of three friends, revolutionaries, Taleno, Jilguero and Indio Larios, who became famous as one of the most wanted men in Nicaragua but actually did very little, spending his days in Guatemala making *piñatas* for children's parties, having lost his stomach for the fight; of the National Guard Colonel, Catalino López, and of many ordinary people, barmen, barflies, guitarists, fishermen, traitors, whores. Vile deeds, such as the bringing of the head of Sandino's general, Pedrón Altamirano, to Managua on the end of a stick, alternated with more comic vilenesses, such as the fixing of the Miss Nicaragua contest of 1953. And behind everything was the malign presence of the tyrant, known only as *el hombre*, the man. To bury one's ancestors in one's own head, in memory, was to confer upon them a kind of immortality, the only kind human beings could offer one another. It was also, of course, to be haunted by their memory for ever.

I was also struck by the reference in the quote from Aristophanes that stood as the novel's epigraph to a time *when the earth did not yet exist*. Here, I thought, was another echo of Uriel Molina's image of Somoza's Nicaragua as captivity, as exile. The Nicaraguan meaning of the Aristophanes quote could only be that in those days the country *wasn't there*. Landless, nationless, the people buried their fathers in themselves, because the self was the only ground they had to stand upon.

As I'd just finished the book, I started asking Sergio Ramírez all the questions that writers get to hate: how real was it? Were the characters drawn from life? 'It's all true,' he told me. 'Everything in the novel comes from actual events.' Ramírez had spent years studying the history of the Sandino period before he wrote the book. 'There really was someone like Indio Larios,' he said. 'Always top of the wanted list, but actually he was never in Nicaragua, he had lost his nerve. And the real Catalino López was a sidekick of Somoza García, a certain Manuel Gómez. But the beating he gets from Jilguero and the others – ' (in the novel, the three friends had captured and humiliated the National Guard officer) ' – that actually happened to a different man. People used to hint that he'd been raped.'

'In the novel, you never quite say what gets done to Catalino.'

'There were many possibilities,' Ramírez said with relish. 'I didn't want to choose. And the other thing that's absolutely true,' he went on, 'is the Miss Nicaragua business.' A certain Miss Bermúdez, daughter of a *Guardia* officer, had been a candidate for the title, and was opposed by a Miss Rosales or Morales. In order to vote you had to clip a coupon from the paper. Miss Bermúdez's candidacy became associated, thanks to her parentage, with the regime, so the people began to vote for her opponent. When *el hombre* heard about this he insisted that Miss Bermúdez must win. His underlings printed quantities of forged entry forms and filled them in with votes for Bermúdez. The whole affair became quite a political hot potato. On the day of the announcement of the result, it was given out that Miss Bermúdez had scraped home. 'Of course everybody knew it had been fixed,' Sergio said. 'Nobody had been voting for her, after all. She would have lost very heavily. So there was uproar. It was too good a story not to use.'

For many years, he said, he had felt a bit of a fraud when people called him a novelist. 'I wrote that book so long ago, and since then it has been mostly political work. I felt as if I were living on my old capital.' But now he was writing a new novel, working every day, for two hours, early in the morning. 'It's the kind of book nobody ever thought I'd write,' he said, happily. 'It's a murder story, based on a famous case of a few years back. Very hot stuff.'

He sounded pleased with his steamy story. 'I've finished a draft,' he said. 'So have I,' I replied gloomily. 'It's taken me three years and I haven't been a vice-president, either.'

Gioconda Belli, the unfairly beautiful poet I'd heard reading at the ruins of the Grand Hotel, arrived with her German publisher and his photographer in tow. I told her I'd read her interview with Margaret Randall. 'Oh,' she said, 'I've changed my mind completely since then.' Then, she had been all for sacrificing her writing to the work of national reconstruction. 'Now I've given up my job to write a novel,' she said. 'My first. It's terrifying.'

I said I had been curious about the relative absence of novelists in this poet-stuffed country. 'There was never time for novels,' she said. 'You could squeeze in poetry between other things. Not a novel.'

So, in spite of all the shortages, there was one commodity that had become a little more plentiful of late: time. Or, perhaps, people had a sense that it might be running out, and were grabbing what remained before it was too late? The photographer was swarming all over Gioconda, photographing her from every conceivable angle. 'So, how has it been?' she asked me.

'I've been taking snapshots, too,' I said. 'There's not much more one can do in a few weeks.'

Snapshot of Gioconda: under Somoza, after she had been recruited by the Frente, she went on working in an advertising agency in Managua, writing copy. I'd done that, too, in my time, and said, 'Oh, good. Somebody else with a shameful past.' The ad-men had never suspected her of a thing. Then the day came when she heard that the authorities were getting on to her, and she left the country at once by a secret safe route to Costa Rica. Two days later, the *Guardia* arrived at the advertising agency to arrest her. Her former colleagues went into deep shock: Gioconda? Impossible, but she was such a nice, pretty girl. The innocence of the salesmen, she said. It had kept her safe for years.

As I was about to leave, I discovered by chance that the English novelist most admired by both Gioconda Belli and Sergio Ramírez was Lawrence Durrell. 'I'd never have guessed that,' I said.

'They don't speak about him in England, I know,' said Gioconda, who had spent time in Suffolk. 'Maybe he's too un-English for the English.' Sergio said he had admired, and been influenced by, Durrell years ago. 'Now I don't dare to re-read him,' he said, 'in case it's not the same.'

On that note, I said goodnight.

'Come back,' Sergio Ramírez said. 'Will you ever come back, do you think?'

'I'll be back.'

Throughout my visit to Nicaragua, amidst all the songs and poetry and prose, I had been plagued by the limerick about the young girl from Nic'ragua, her jaguar ride, and the transferred smile. It had been infuriating, at times, like a jingle that refused to be forgotten. That last night, the thing invaded my dreams; or, rather, the smile did, the smile on the face of the jaguar, except that there wasn't any face. I was pursued across an amorphous, shifting landscape by that lethal rictus which one might have likened to the grin of the Cheshire Cat had it not been for the teeth, which were long, curved and melodramatically dripping with blood. I ran for my life across my dream, chased by the jaguar smile.

I woke up in a jumble of nightmare, limerick and sweat. As I lay awake and calmed down, it occurred to me that the limerick, when applied to contemporary Nicaragua, was capable of both a conservative and a radical reading, that there were, so to speak, two limericks, two Misses Nicaragua riding two jaguars, and it was necessary to vote for the version one preferred. If the young girl was taken to be the revolution, seven years old, fresh, still full of the idealism of youth, then the jaguar was geopolitics, or the United States; after all, an attempt to create a free country where there had been, for half a century, a colonized 'back yard', and to do so when you were weak and the enemy close to omnipotent, was indeed to ride a jaguar. That was the 'leftist' interpretation; but what if the young girl were Nicaragua itself, and the jaguar was the revolution? Eh? What about that?

I closed my eyes and looked through my collection of Nicaraguan snapshots. Finally I chose between the two girls on the two jaguars. I tore up the picture that looked, well, *wrong*, and threw it away. In the one I preserved, the girl on the jaguar looked like the Mona Lisa, smiling her Gioconda smile.

As I drove to the airport the next morning, the posters of Managua said goodbye. 'Tuberculosis can be cured!' 'Conservatism is the Family'. 'Death to the yankee invader!' 'K-Othrine

Insecticide'. 'Conservatism is Respect for the Church'. 'Discover the Baha'i Faith'.

Daniel Ortega was on the car radio, speaking at the UN Security Council. At translation speed, he was asking for international law to be upheld, insisting upon Nicaragua's right to self-determination. Nicaragua against the United States, Daniel against Goliath. The International Court's judgment was the stone in his sling.

The mouse roared.

My internal dispute hadn't ended. I thought the Sandinistas were, in a way, elitists. They believed they had been tempered by the fires of the revolution, they had become 'new men', and at times, no doubt, they felt that only those who had passed through the fire were fitted to rule. But the inescapable fact was that, whatever Violeta de Chamorro claimed, they had come to power through the ballot box, and were the legitimate rulers of the land.

Some of them probably were 'communists', even 'Marxist-Leninists'. (Although the leaders I met seemed far from being ideologues.) But if Nicaragua was a Soviet-style state, I was a monkey's uncle.

I had also come to respect the government's political skill, its will, and its integrity. J.K. Galbraith had written, in a recent *Herald Tribune* essay, about 'sleaze' and the Reagan administration. Once, he said, American men who had money had sought public office. Now men who had public office sought money. 'I prefer the earlier motivation,' he remarked.

It was hard to believe that such an administration could claim moral superiority over the likes of Miguel d'Escoto.

Ortega was still speaking on the radio. I recalled asking him why he thought the US had such a bee in its bonnet about Nicaragua. He had replied: 'It isn't only us. What Reagan wants to do, by defeating us, is to send a message to the region.'

The message of the FSLN's overthrow would be loud and clear: give up, folks. Accept that you belong to the American empire. Resistance is useless; you only end up worse off than you were to begin with. 'Just do as we say.'

'That is why,' Ortega had said, 'we believe we are fighting for the whole of Central America. We are fighting to say, this is not somebody else's back yard. This is our country.'

Perhaps David and Goliath was the wrong metaphor. Perhaps Nicaragua's struggle was better compared to that of the ancient Gauls in the famous French comic-books by Goscinny and Uderzo: Astérix, Obélix and the rest, holding out in their tiny enclave against the might of Jules César and his Romans. As I listened to Ortega on the radio, I invented a new Gaul: Sandinix.

The morning paper had brought the news of a Contra attack. Five men had been killed in Jinotega province, at a place called Zompopera. Three of them had been Nicaraguans: William Blandón and Mario Acevedo of the FSLN, and a naturalized Frenchman, Joel Flueux. The others were a Swiss citizen, Claude Leyvraz, and Bernd Erich Koversteyn, from West Germany. (As a result of these killings the Nicaraguan government later banned all foreign volunteer workers from the war zone, one of the saddest pieces of news I heard after my return. Later still, the Contra leadership announced, presumably with the blessing of the US, that from now on any foreign aid workers found in the war zone would be treated as enemy agents.)

Daniel Ortega finished pleading for justice at the UN, while, without his knowing it, the dance of death in Nicaragua took another of its slow, grave steps.

SILVIA: AN EPILOGUE

On the plane home I sat beside a Nicaraguan woman with a soft face, thick spectacles and a streaming cold. She was married to a Frenchman and now lived in Paris. We spoke in French, and I soon realized that she was in a distraught state.

I had asked her if she returned to Nicaragua often. (She had left just before the '72 earthquake, so that 'her' Managua had largely vanished. Only the photograph of old Managua at the Los Antojitos café really reminded her of home.)

'Yes,' she said, 'my mother lives there, I just went to visit her, but two days before I arrived she, she, died.' She began to weep, then controlled herself as if bored by her tears. 'They kept the body until I came.' I made inadequate noises, how tragic, how did it happen, you must feel awful.

She felt her mother's medical treatment had not been up to the mark. The cause of death had been a thrombosis, a huge clot in a major artery, but radiology had failed to detect anything; they hadn't seen the clot. 'They said the picture wasn't clear. Some equipment, some fluids were lacking, because of the shortages, the economic blockade by the US.'

Silvia blamed the government. 'I come from a Sandinista family. Both my brothers are active in the Frente, also before the triumph. But now I go back and I see the same old habits of the Somoza time creeping back.'

For instance? 'For example, there was an arts and crafts exhibit at the ruins of the Grand Hotel. The first day it was not open to the public, but by invitation only. The second day, you found out that all the best pieces had already been reserved. That was how Hope Somoza used to behave.'

'Yes, I see,' I said, not having expected so sudden a change of subject.

'Also the prices of primitive paintings have gone through the roof,' she said. 'And the transport system in Managua is appalling.'

I asked if her husband had ever been to Nicaragua. 'Yes,' Silvia said, 'but there is the problem of the expense of the air tickets, and besides it is hard to bring my whole family; one simply cannot find *domestiques*, and there are no automatic washing machines, one must wash everything by hand, and there is the ironing, and the cooking, and everything.'

She was a good-hearted woman, in spite of the sound of the above. She had trained as an architect and had gone to Europe to complete her studies. 'Everyone told me I'd never come back. I had dreamed for years of being in all that grandeur, all that splendour of buildings. But I never thought I'd stay away. Then things happened very quickly, and I was married, and there it was.'

Did she have a vote in Nicaragua? No, she said, she lived abroad, but her family had all voted for the Frente. 'And now?' I asked. 'Would they vote for the Frente again, or have they changed their minds?'

'No, no, they haven't,' she said. 'But things are wrong, everybody knows that.'

She opposed the closure of *La Prensa* and thought, as I did, that *Barricada* was the most boring paper she'd ever seen. She felt the FSLN leaders didn't really understand why the freedom of the press was so important. 'They are boys, who went from school to the mountains to jail or into exile. Are they really properly prepared for the running of a State?' And then, in another of her vertiginous non sequiturs: 'Taxi drivers in Managua these days! They charge the earth. There is supposed to be a rate, but they ignore it, and there is nothing anyone can do. Nothing. It's wrong.'

As she dozed, wisps of Nicaragua floated through my mind in the eddying, repetitious fashion of airplane thoughts. How isolated from information it was. 'England?' a *campesino* asked me, and then struggled to offer some piece of knowledge about the place. *'Sí, sí: Reina Isabel, no?'* And India, to most Nicaraguans, always excepting the followers of Rabindranath, seemed an exotic, camelious, elephantine place; they were amazed when I drew parallels between that fantasyland and their own country. And yet those parallels did exist. The three tendencies of the FSLN, for example, echoed the divisions and arguments in the Indian left, and in many other poor countries of the South. There were also differences. India was poorer than Nicaragua, but not nearly so information-poor. Very little foreign news made the pages of *Barricada* and *El Nuevo Diario* during my stay. 'Torrijos was assassinated by the CIA.' 'US, UK spy on ANC for South Africa.' 'Royal wedding stages a distraction from the quarrel between Reina Isabel and Mrs Thatcher.' That was about it.

To tell the truth, Nicaraguans didn't seem perturbed by the absence of the world. Their own circumstances absorbed them so deeply that they had little room left for curiosity. Very few people asked me any questions, though they were all happy to answer mine. History was roaring in their ears, deafening them to more distant noises.

'History,' in Veronica Wedgwood's phrase, 'is lived forward but it is written in retrospect.' To live in the real world was to act without knowing the end. The act of living a real life differed, I mused, from the act of making a fictional one, too, because you were stuck with your mistakes. No revisions, no second drafts. To visit Nicaragua was to be shown that the world was not television, or history, or fiction. The world was real, and this was its actual, unmediated reality.

I had left Nicaragua unfinished, so to speak, a country in which the ancient, opposing forces of creation and destruction were in violent collision. The fashionable pessimism of our age suggested that the destroyers would always, in the end, prove stronger than the creators, and, indeed, those who would unmake the Nicaraguan revolution were men of awesome power. The new weapons of the counter-revolution, purchased with the US dollars, were moving into place; soon it would be time for battle. The logic of *realpolitik* said that there could only be one result: now that the US had opted for a straightforward military solution in Nicaragua, its might would eventually prevail. But that kind of logic had proved fallible in the past. Unhappy endings might seem more realistic than happy ones, but reality often contained a streak of fantasy that realism (*pace* Tagore) lacked. In the real world, there were monsters and giants; but there was also the immeasurable power of the will. It was entirely possible that Nicaragua's will to survive might prove stronger than the American weapons. We would just have to see.

❧

'One worries for the future,' Silvia said after a time. 'Because if the Contra come to power the Sandinistas will go into the mountains and become guerrillas again, so it's endless, no?' I suggested that if the revolution managed to outlast Reagan, his successor might follow a different line, and without US support the Contra weren't much to worry about. She looked dubious but was too polite to disagree openly. 'It's possible, what you say,' she said, without conviction.

I asked my well-worn question: 'What do you think the government should do, then? Should it try and make peace with the Americans?'

'You said "Americans",' she reproached me.

'I'm sorry. North Americans. Unitedstatesians. Reaganians. Them.'

'It's all right,' she forgave me quickly. 'When I first came to Europe from Nicaragua, it would shock me to hear the US called "America". I wanted to protest, But *we* are America, not just them. But now I say it too: America, Americans. Europe teaches you a different perspective.'

'Yes,' I agreed, 'it certainly does.'

She went back to my question. 'No, they can't give in. The war must go on. It's difficult to know what to do. The revolution exists. It has to exist, or there's no hope. But what problems! What difficulties! What grief!'

She had started crying again, and was fighting against it. I pretended to think it was just her heavy cold.

I was surprised and touched by the force of what she'd said, this sweet middle-class woman with her affluent complaints, whose mother might have lived if it hadn't been for the shortages. *'It has to exist, or there's no hope.'*

❧

We parted in Madrid, and returned to our separate lives, two migrants making our way in this West stuffed with money, power and things, this North that taught us how to see from its privileged point of view. But maybe we were the lucky ones; we knew that other perspectives existed. We had seen the view from elsewhere.

ACKNOWLEDGEMENTS

The translations on pages 6–7, 10–11, 28, 30–31, and 89 are taken from *Nicaragua in Revolution: The Poets Speak*, ed. Aldaraca, Baker, Rodríguez and Zimmerman, MEP Publications, Minneapolis (with, in some cases, some small changes made by myself); that on page 22 from *Nicaragua in Reconstruction and at War*, ed. Marc Zimmerman, MEP Publications. I have also quoted from *Risking a Somersault in the Air: Conversations with Nicaraguan Writers*, by Margaret Randall, Solidarity Publications.

I should like to thank all those, in London and in Nicaragua, who gave me invaluable assistance and advice, most particularly Nicaragua's Ambassador to the UK, H.E. Francisco d'Escoto; Biddy Richards; my interpreter, Margarita Clark; and, of course, Sra. Rosario Murillo and the ASTC.

I can find no adequate words of thanks for the hospitality I was shown by the people of Nicaragua.

—S.R.